Praise for *U*

"In *Unsatisfied: Finding Contentn.*

Ann Sullivan accomplishes something I wish could be taught yet fear that it can't: She writes an in-your-face book about a deeply difficult subject, yet she avoids preaching. Rather, Ann takes a come-alongside approach and shares her life, warts and all, revealing what she's learned and how she's grown—allowing us to apply the morals and principles for ourselves. It's a work of art."

—**Jerry B. Jenkins**, novelist and biographer, The Jerry Jenkins Writers Guild

"Ann is an incredibly gifted communicator who is able to take timeless principles and make them accessible to everyone. With both humor and insight, her new book, *Unsatisfied*, will inspire, encourage, and equip Christians in the marketplace and beyond."

—**Bob Lambert**, founding partner, Samurai Business Group LLC and radio talk show host at Faith Marketplace

"Ann tackles the topic of contentment with an honesty and humor that makes it easy to read, while chocked full of good-sense advice. Using stories from her own life as her 'teaching tool,' she gives practical advice without pretending to have easy answers. And she does all this without laying any guilt trips on those of us who still struggle with finding contentment in a discontented world. This is an issue common to many, and it will help any who read it with open hearts and minds."

—**Mary Whelchel Lowman**, speaker and founder, The Christian Working Woman

"With refreshing humor and insight, Ann skillfully weaves together timeless principles and the current issues of life. She points to all the things we should be grateful for and the disappointments that keep us from celebrating. If you're ready for an honest look at our struggle and the practical solutions that are available, you'll want to pick up Ann Sullivan's book, *Unsatisfied*."

—**Leslie Strobel**, coauthor of *Spiritual Mismatch*

"Ann Sullivan knows how to connect with her audiences, both as a speaker and as an author. In her latest book, *Unsatisfied*, Ann takes an unflinching look at our search for contentment. She offers examples of our struggle and insight for overcoming the battle. I highly recommend you get a copy for yourself and anyone else you might know who might be in the fight."

—**Joyce Oglesby**, host of *The Just Ask Joyce Show*

ANN C. SULLIVAN

UN
SATIS
FIED

Finding Contentment
in a
Discontented
World

ABINGDON PRESS
NASHVILLE

For my kids.

CONTENTS

Chapter One

THE
BATTLE
BEGINS

When I agreed to speak at a women's conference out West on the topic of contentment, I had no idea I'd be battling depression. If I'd known, I would've thought twice about committing.

Choosing a topic for a bunch of strangers is tricky business even without depression. It's even trickier when a coordinator wants me to announce my topic months before I'm ready to pick one. I've actually received publicity brochures in the mail detailing my talks long before I've written them. I'll read the descriptions and think, *Hmm, I'd like to hear that.*

I love connecting with women, but when I land at a

> *I'm not even sure I knew what hope was until I lost it. Before then, life was full of possibilities.*

retreat, I'm typically going in blind. I'll stand at the podium and look out over the sea of unfamiliar faces and think, *I wonder what they're all retreating from.* Would they tell me stories of cruddy jobs or cranky spouses? Would they tell me how tough it was just getting away for the weekend? Or would they tell me it's a great day, and they're ready to celebrate the good things in life, like caramel lattés and girlfriends?

What kids?

One thing I can count on, though, wherever I'm booked to speak, the moment a topic is chosen, I know I'm going to get worked over by it, just a bit. It's God's way of keeping me real and giving me something worthwhile to say to the strangers who are obviously not strangers to Him.

And it happens every time. If I'm speaking on the topic of contentment, I suddenly have none. If I'm speaking on discernment, I can't figure anything out. If I'm asked to address the power of self-control, I become the kitchen magnet that reads, "Lead me not into temptation, I can find it myself."

A few years ago, for instance, my kids were driving me crazy right around the time I was asked to speak at a moms' event at a large contemporary church. I sat at my computer trying to come up with some sort of outline that would inspire young moms, but all I could come up with was:

1. Don't have any more kids.
2. Quit while you're ahead.
3. Bigger kids, bigger problems.
(Let's close in prayer.)

Depression can show up very quickly, usually after a crisis. But for me, depression crept up almost imperceptibly, generously offering a front row seat to the world of discontentment. All the things that used to bring me pleasure suddenly offered none. I'm not even sure I knew what hope was until I lost it. Before then, life was full of possibilities.

Then one day, while he was home from college and grabbing milk from the fridge, my son suddenly stopped and looked at me and said, "Mom, you gotta get a grip."

That's when I realized I'd been crying for six months. Maybe I did have a problem.

This Could Be Trouble

Not that a person needs to be depressed to feel discontent. For me, though, depression and discontentment fit together beautifully. They bonded instantly. Depression became rocket fuel for my discontentment, exposing every unsatisfied inch of my life. Then, to make matters worse, guilt showed up. I knew I should be grateful. Clearly, I had more than some. But those thoughts didn't help. They only irritated me more.

It was all very unpleasant, but I will say this: going through the process taught me something very interesting about unhappy people. Like it or not, we can be extremely self-absorbed. Discontentment often signals an unhealthy preoccupation with one's self (although that preoccupation can be a good thing if it helps us recognize areas of our lives that need improvement).

After my depression lifted, I went through a kind of honeymoon period where nothing seemed to bother me. Life was good. I felt immune to problems. It was like the rush of new love—the kind I watched a boy have for my daughter right around that same time.

One evening, braving a particularly treacherous snowstorm, he appeared at our front door shivering from head to toe. The poor lovesick kid. He was in school full-time and worked lots of hours, but somehow, he was always at our house. I'm not sure when he slept. As he kicked off his shoes, I felt compelled to warn him that my daughter had been nursing a head cold. She was a walking petri dish. It wasn't pretty. She'd been carrying around a box of tissues with her all day . . . wandering from room to room, infecting every doorknob.

But the boy only smiled, shrugged his shoulders, and said, "I don't care." Then he bolted down to the TV room, leaping three steps at a time, where he found my daughter wrapped in a quilt and blowing her nose.

I stood there for a moment wondering what becomes of

those delirious days of new love. After thirty years of marriage, when my husband or I catch a cold, we stack enough pillows between us to reach the ceiling. I'm not sure of the science behind it, but we figure if we can't stop the germs altogether, maybe we can disorient them.

When my depression ended, I became the emotional equivalent of a star-crossed newlywed—all sweetness and smiles. But eventually I sensed the honeymoon coming to an end. As life came back into focus, I found myself counting the cost of what I'd just been through.

Maybe I'd need to rethink this thing called contentment, even though I'd been speaking on it for years. Maybe I'd need to revisit the Bible verse I'd always wanted to believe: "Delight yourself in the Lord, and He will give you the desires of your heart" (Psalm 37:4 ESV).

What did that even mean?

I suddenly realized how weary I'd become of platitudes and promises that felt empty. I'd grown skeptical of altar calls, emotional conversions, and, yes, self-help books. Those things may work for some but never have for me.

I was finding emotions to be highly unreliable. When stretched to the limit, they can make us see things and feel things that aren't even real. In contrast, the faith I was discovering in Scripture was deeper than that, grittier, and meant for the long haul. It was levelheaded and bolstered by reliable standards, like cutting-edge research and Harvard studies.

I'd already moved past the gaping hole that atheism had

created in me, along with the nagging suspicion that *if* God was there He probably didn't care. Still, I wanted to be clear about what I could expect from Him in terms of contentment. And what did He expect from me? Because even on our best days, when we're not facing divorce, job loss, or bankruptcy, life can still be tough.

Programmed for Problems

If we want to clear a path to a lasting contentment, figuring out why we struggle in the first place becomes really important. We need to see the obstacles before we can clear them. Sometimes the reasons are obvious, like searchlights in a black sky pointing out a potential shipwreck. Other times the reasons are subtle, slithering quietly into our lives like a poisonous snake waiting to strike. And the reasons are different for everyone, beginning with the fact that some of us just seem to be born more content than others. It's the gene pool we swim in.

When my son was little, I'd stick him in a stroller, hand him a cracker, and we'd spend hours walking through the mall. He'd amuse himself with my car keys or the mirror in the fitting room while I tried on a pile of sundresses. But when my daughter came along, she wouldn't stay in the stroller if her life depended on it, which it usually did by the end of our outing. I never knew why, and I'm not sure she did either, but like all discontented people, she just wanted *out*. Anyplace seemed better than where she was.

We didn't see the mall for two years.

When my niece, a mother of four, was pregnant with her first, like most new moms, she wanted to do everything by the book. She kept handy her copy of *What to Expect When You're Expecting* and did her best to create a womb full of happiness. She watched her diet, got plenty of exercise, avoided chemicals and undue stress. Nevertheless, when she gave birth, her beautiful newborn spent what felt like the entire first year of her life crying.

Sure, there were plenty of theories: an underdeveloped digestive system, sensitivity to hot and cold, a full moon. But no one ever really figured out why.

Then, right about the time things quieted down, my niece announced she was pregnant again. We held our collective breath. This time, though, she said she'd be doing things differently. She'd take it down a notch and enjoy juicy cheeseburgers, peanut M&Ms, and maybe even a glass of wine when the doctor said it was safe. And call it a coincidence, but when that little guy popped out, he was smiling, confirming the age-old saying, "If mama ain't happy, ain't nobody happy."

Life in the Bubble

The personalities we're born with make a huge difference in how we process life. So does the environment we're brought up in. When my kids were growing up, they knew nothing of alcoholism, abuse, or dysfunction. When I was young, I didn't know those things existed either. Remarkably, my mom would tell you the same thing about her childhood.

That's *three* generations of bubble-wrapped living!

My mom's bubble was still intact even in her early teens. She was helping teach a Sunday school class and noticed a little boy who came in with a black eye. As he walked by, my mom asked what happened. Almost in passing, he answered, "My dad hit me."

My mom just assumed the boy was kidding. The idea that parents might actually harm their own children was so foreign to her, his words didn't even register. Later, though, when she learned some parents do hurt their kids, the boy's face began to haunt her. She never forgot it.

It's a painful moment when we discover how tough the world can be, especially when we're playing nice and following the rules. After years of living in my delightful bubble, I made up for lost time when I developed a nasty panic disorder in college. It dug its claws into my life and tormented me for thirteen years.

My home life was great, but college life was even better. Frat houses. Designer jeans. Really cute boys. But happy hour came to a screeching halt the moment I had my first panic attack. I was terrified and became desperate for answers when everything I thought I knew suddenly shifted.

What was wrong with me? And where was God?

Several doctors, counselors, and pastors later, I finally found my answers. And looking back now, I can see the purpose of my struggle. It had a very refining impact on me and changed the trajectory of my life. (Easy to say now.) It also taught me that even in our worst moments, God still has our back. And when we learn how to recognize the bad things for what they are, the better we can become at maximizing the good.

The Expert

Struggling with a panic disorder made me more of an expert on anxiety, depression, and despair than I ever cared to be. You become a "scholar" in one of two ways: in the classroom or in the trenches. I spent plenty of time in both. By now, you could say I'm a bit of an authority when it comes to fear and doubt.

For years I lived with my humiliating affliction and just assumed I was one of "those" people. Not too strong. Not too bright. Then, when I was finally diagnosed and treated by a very heads-up internist, I realized I wasn't crazy. I wasn't weak either. In fact, my doctor told me it was quite the opposite. He said it had taken enormous strength to press through my panic disorder the way I did. And now, if I can give that same encouragement to someone else who's struggling, well, it almost makes the pain worthwhile.

I survived because I had a solid support system in place, and I opted for healthier solutions, like jogging rather than drinking. But it was always a battle. And when I finally learned there wasn't anything *really* wrong with me, it was like meeting myself for the first time.

We create all sorts of false narratives in our lives, and it's natural to assume the worst about ourselves when we're struggling. We wonder if we brought the problems on ourselves or if maybe we could have avoided them somehow.

And negative thoughts can be addicting. All those creative brain cells, the ones that used to be so helpful, suddenly turn on us. The chemicals get out of balance and the synapse wires get crossed.

But our struggle doesn't necessarily mean there's something wrong with us. It could just mean there's something wrong with the way we've been doing things. And if what we're doing isn't working—n*ews flash!*—it's time to try something else.

Heartburn

Most of us live our lives somewhere between completely clueless and totally overwhelmed. Understanding where we come from and what's going on around us is an important part of our personal equation. This is the kind of information we need if we're ready to chart a new course.

Twenty years of working with women has shown me lots

of ways behaviors are learned or inherited. Our tendencies toward depression and anxiety are often genetic, whereas resentment and intolerance are typically modeled. Understanding our own dynamics

Life is a journey, and contentment is all about heading in the right direction.

of "nature vs. nurture" can give us an entirely new set of tools to work with as we confront our discontent.

I've heard Woody Allen talk about our need for the power of distraction. "The best you can do to get through life is distraction.... The key is to distract yourself."[1] A new romance, a good movie, a creative moment, Allen says we can distract ourselves in a "billion" different ways.

At first, I used to view Allen's comments as negative— almost futile. Then, after processing a little more life, I found myself rethinking his words. Perhaps I'd been a bit hasty.

For some, discontentment will come and go like heartburn after a spicy taco. But for those of us who battle stubborn moments of discontentment and unhappiness, Allen's advice is insightful. A good distraction may be all the antacid we need. Finding things that can distract us, preferably things that are healthy and legal, may be all we need to pull our minds out of their temporary funk.

And it should be something fun—or at least useful. Something that will pay dividends later, such as when I first started blogging. I thought, *Who besides my mother will even see this?* But it kept me busy, and two years later I had fabulous material for a second book.

Here's the thing. Life is a journey, and contentment is all about heading in the right direction. Happiness is a byproduct of doing the right thing, though there's no guarantee that every step of the journey will *feel* good. Sometimes we need to get comfortable with being uncomfortable, at least for a while. For most of us, anxiety, anger, or sadness will come and go. But if we're on the right track, we'll eventually get where we need to go.

Empty Spaces

Discontentment not only exposes our weaknesses but also reveals the empty places inside of us. Learning to fill those spaces with good things is an important life skill for people who struggle with discontent. But again, the art of "healthy diversion" comes easier to some than others.

My husband has always been good at puttering. Instead of stewing over a disappointment, he finds a project to busy himself with while he processes his pain. The result is usually something we all benefit from, like updated landscaping, a new ceiling, or his famous raspberry jam.

The differences between his "tendencies" and mine became glaringly apparent several years ago. After decades of living in large houses with big closets and oversized bathrooms, it was time to start thinking about downsizing.

The handwriting was on the wall. Our nation's financial bubble had burst, our kids were in college, and the tax rates in Illinois continued to increase whether our square footage was being used or not.

We figured it would take a while for our house to sell, so we put it on the market right away—long before I was ready. And wouldn't you know, the thing sold immediately, which thrilled my husband but left me feeling homeless.

Technically, we were homeless, for a few months, as we looked at houses and even considered renting. But nothing appealed to me. Because the truth is, I wasn't ready to downsize my house, my family, or anything else in my life. So, while I busied myself with bitterness and self-pity, my husband took the reins and talked me into a modest short sale that was in desperate need of repair.

I cringed as the Realtor walked us through the place, but the skilled handyman in my husband glowed with the possibilities. In the days and weeks that followed, I watched him channel his inner Chip and Joanna, knocking down walls and yanking up floorboards. He completely transformed the place and was energized by every upgrade he made. Not only would the little house be cozy and affordable with its huge tax reduction but would also sell quickly when the time was right.

But for me, the entire process only exposed my own moldy floorboards. My sense of contentment was constantly tested as I tried to adjust to small spaces and virtually no storage. And I failed miserably at it. I remember wondering how it was I'd become so spoiled. I thought I was a generous person. I thought I was a grateful person. I knew I was better off than most, though I've never understood why we should find solace in knowing that others have it worse than we do. Maybe I needed to learn a few things about being generous and taking fewer things for granted. Like my taste buds, which I always tend to forget about until I'm stuffed up with a head cold and lose all sense of taste and smell. It's then that I come to appreciate those little buds that cover my tongue, the ones I forgot are there.

I tried very hard to remain open and teachable as each wall of entitlement came crashing down around me. And, eventually, I made a startling discovery. Downsizing was far more liberating than I ever thought it could be. In fact, it seemed that the more stuff I got rid of, the clearer my head became. It was like coming home from the dentist after a good flossing and cleaning. But it also left me wondering how many other areas of my life needed the same kind of attention. Maybe there were better ways to look at my disappointments.

Equal Opportunity Offender

Another interesting factoid about discontentment is that it doesn't discriminate. Recently I read an NPR article on immigrants desperate to reach American soil. They, too, want the opportunity to find contentment and live out the

American Dream, though that dream seems to have taken a bit of a hit.

The article pointed out that for the first time in decades, life expectancy in America has dipped. And the new demographic most at risk? Surprisingly, white middle-aged men—the group that has typically had the edge in recent decades.

Shocked by the statistics, Princeton researchers explored the findings, and what they discovered was unsettling. The mortality rate in the United States had been falling by 2 percent annually since the 1970s. But an uptick in suicide among middle-aged white men, mainly due to drug and alcohol abuse, had changed the numbers. The newest drug of choice was coming from the opioid family, specifically prescription painkillers. And while the researchers didn't necessarily think the medical community was intentionally playing fast and loose with our discomfort, the potential for abuse was staggering, especially for those whose pain extended beyond their bodies.

Usually when we think about mood swings or insecurities, we picture sulking, angst-ridden teenagers. But according to the article, it's their fathers we should perhaps start worrying about. Also, the researchers discovered that this troubling trend isn't seen in the African American or Hispanic communities. It's mainly in the Caucasian population.

"Something's clearly going wrong with this age group in America," says John Haaga, director of social research at the National Institute on Aging.[2]

Professor Jon Skinner of Dartmouth has offered an interesting take on these statistics too. One explanation is that things had been going well for white men and their parents in America, but then the bubble burst. The financial floor dropped out in 2008, and expectations were left unmet. But for nonwhite households, things had never been that optimistic in the first place, according to Skinner, so maybe that's why the disappointment among that demographic wasn't as great.

As I read the article, I wasn't sure which part of Skinner's comments were more troubling—the fact that white middle-aged men have taken a major hit, including the white middle-aged man I was married to, or that nonwhite men live without optimism.

And what exactly is the moral to this story, if there is one? Should we aim low in life to avoid disappointment? This kind of talk is hardly the stuff motivational speeches are made of. What sells books and fills stadiums are the pearly white smiles of speakers who collectively tell us to set the bar higher. But aren't unmet expectations what get us in trouble in the first place?

For many, the American Dream has morphed from humble gratitude to insatiable demand. I've seen it happen to others, and I've seen it happen to me. Much more was renovated than our little short sale.

Chapter Two

TOO
MUCH
DRAMA

Years ago, I read a little book called *We Are Driven*. In it the author said our "insatiable desire" to do more, have more, and be more is one of the most predominant emotional illnesses of our time. Nothing is ever quite enough.

Sound familiar?

I think discontented people live in a kind of holding pattern when it comes to contentment . . . circling the airport but never quite landing. We're convinced life will begin for us when:

> we lose ten pounds.
> we get that promotion.
> we have another baby.

(Or, at the other end of the
spectrum: when baby finally
moves out.)

There's nothing wrong with all this good stuff. I like the extra money in the bank, the upgrades to the kitchen, and the "all clear" from the doctor. I like it when my husband comes home from work and tells me he just won a trip for two to Maui through his job . . . and he wants to take me. That's good stuff.

The problem is, sometimes there is no remodeled kitchen. There's no new baby or clean bill of health. Sometimes there's no trip for two to Maui won by a husband through his job. Sometimes there's no job. Sometimes there's no husband.

This is where we live. This is where discontentment takes root, and we begin to wonder about ourselves, other people, and God. This is when our discontentment becomes that annoying kid in the pool who yells, "Watch me!" every ten seconds.

But here's the thing about the kid in the pool: sometimes we need to pay attention, even if it's just to shut him up. My struggle signaled the need for medical attention. After thirteen years of battling my panic disorder, it responded well to medication. And for some, that will be their solution too.

It's good to live in a time when medication is available. There should be no shame in taking meds. And while there's always opportunity for abuse, a powerful case can be made for how neglecting medication is just as reckless as taking too much. It's hard to believe there are still people who disapprove of the responsible use of meds. They pass quiet (or not-so-quiet) judgment on those who use them. Most of the harsh naysayers I've run into are people who've never dealt with serious anxiety or depression. (Though, if there's any real justice in the universe, maybe someday they will.) They declare medication to be a sign of weakness or, worse yet, a lack of faith. *Don't even get me started.*

> *Disconnected people live in a kind of holding pattern when it comes to contentment . . . circling the airport but never quite landing.*

Comedian Chonda Pierce once said,

> A woman came to me after a show and said, "I don't think you should talk about taking antidepressants. It makes your faith look weak!" I said to her very candidly, "Then you should take your glasses off and drive home! Where's your faith?"[1]

Our brain is like any other organ in our body and can get strained or sick. Making someone feel guilty about it only stresses him or her further. Should we withhold insulin from a diabetic or ridicule that person because his or her pancreas doesn't work? I've seen firsthand the carnage that results from withholding medication from someone who needs it. With nowhere else to turn, self-medicating feels like their only real option, and the fallout can be devastating.

I probably would have survived without meds, but I certainly wouldn't have thrived the way I did, nor would I have reached my potential. It's not easy trying to talk someone out of clinical depression. It doesn't respond well to "Buck up!" or "Snap out of it!" It's like having the flu for months. You want to peel yourself off the couch and take a shower, but just thinking about it is exhausting.

I could tell my depression was lessening by the growing timespan between each bout of tears. Also, I was starting to enjoy the little things in life again, like a steaming cup of coffee in the morning and my freshly washed sheets at night. It was the hours in between that were still giving me trouble.

Seasons of Struggle

Each stage of life brings with it its own kind of discontentment. I had my first midlife crisis when I turned thirty. My second came at forty. So by the time I turned fifty, I was *really* good at it. By then I'd handled just enough life to realize that we all have "something" that challenges our balance. Younger women are trying to figure things out. Older women begin to fear it's too late. Single women want to be married. Married women want to be single. Stay-at-home moms want to go to work. Working women want to stay home.

When I was a young mom, I remember older women

admiring my babies and telling me to savor every moment with them. "Nibble on those cheeks and toes!" they'd say, reminding me that time passes too quickly.

Too quickly?

Their words usually had the reverse effect on me as I struggled to make it to nap time. But now that I'm older and my kids are grown, I realize they were right. I catch myself reminding other young moms to nibble on their babies' toes too. Because, believe me, those precious toes will lose their charm very quickly.

I'm edging into the "older woman" category faster than I'd care to, though I'm discovering it's not all bad. For one thing, they're right when they say, "As you age, you get more comfortable in your skin." This is true, I discovered, and well timed since you tend to accumulate more of it.

All the jokes about getting older are starting to make sense now too. Like, you know you're getting older when your secrets are safe with your friends because they can't remember them either. Or, after fifty you're still hot, only now it comes in flashes.

My girlfriends are great at finding funny birthday cards to lighten the mood and soften the blow of another year.

My favorite card cuts to the chase and simply says, "I went to buy something special to wear to your birthday party, and the clerk told me the current fashions are big, baggy, and wrinkled. So, I'm coming naked." One of the more disconcerting things about aging is the first time you look in the mirror and see your mother's face. (Or mistake an old friend for her mother.) By my forties, I began losing interest in mirror-gazing, which I'd done far too much of anyway. It seemed more suited for the young . . . and not just for girls, mind you.

One of the things I like most about outdoor running is not having to worry about what I look like sweating at the gym in front of a lot of young men. Then one day I realized that the massive mirrors lining the place kept those boys far too occupied with their own reflection for them to worry about me. It was kind of liberating . . . a good news/bad news scenario, I guess. The good news is they didn't notice me. The bad news is they didn't notice me.

We work hard to feel good about ourselves, and I'm all for it. But here's the thing: unless we're competing for Miss America or a place on the runway, I'm not sure people really notice a few pounds here or a deep line there. But right about the time those fine lines around the eyes become prominent, our friends can't see them anyway without reading glasses.

People tend to see us the way we've always been to them. And no matter how good or bad we look, personality completely takes over after the first few moments of interaction.

Ticking . . .

Still, that first tinge of panic we feel when we realize we're not getting any younger is a little frightening. The kids are growing, the parents are aging, and time is getting away from us. It's like a mudslide . . . there's no slowing down, and there's no turning back, though some people refuse to believe it.

As I felt myself growing older, I told myself the last thing I wanted to do was become one of those women whose desperation is planted all over her tightly stretched face. The truth is, I've always admired the lines of a seasoned woman who's secure in herself.

When I first read the Genesis story of Potiphar's wife, the original cougar, and how she came on to Joseph, a young man at the time, I thought . . . *Eww*. But now, with a few years under my belt, I can see her story from a different angle. Maybe she was feeling empty, unimportant, or that life was passing her by.

I know what it's like for life to become routine and disappointing. I've also come to appreciate the beauty of youth. I'm always pointing out cute boys to my daughter. These days they seem to be everywhere. But my daughter just rolls her eyes and reminds me that if I were twenty, I wouldn't find them so attractive.

I suppose she's right, though I'm not sure who her comment offends more, me or the boys. But I can say this for a fact: I know how to spot a desperate woman when I see one. I know what a selfish woman looks like too—one who's so focused on getting her own needs met that she doesn't care how she hurts the people around her.

Maybe life as the wife of the captain of the palace guard had grown mundane. Maybe Mrs. Potiphar was tired of sitting around waiting for her husband to give her the attention she craved. Whatever the reason, she set her sights on Joseph, who must have been one nice-looking guy. Genesis 39:6 describes him as "well-built and handsome."

I began praying for opportunities to serve others and find amazing fulfillment in that.

Now, at the risk of sounding uber-spiritual, I'll tell you something I did in my forties that was quite wise, if I may say so. During one midlife crisis, I had the good sense to begin shifting my focus away from the things I couldn't hold on to. It wasn't easy, and it did involve a bit of grieving. But hope showed up as I began asking God to help me age gracefully, love more intentionally, and discover brand-new ways to be fulfilled. I began praying for opportunities to serve others and find amazing fulfillment in that. And guess what? God must like those kinds of prayers.

Midlife Madness

I met a new friend for coffee at a cute café, and it was one of those electric conversations. You know the kind, where you're fifteen minutes in before you realize you haven't ordered anything yet.

She's a beautiful bundle of energy, and as I listened to

her all-too-familiar story, I was reminded of how often we're caught off guard by midlife. I mean, we know it's coming, but are we really prepared? I'm not saying we should live our lives as though we're crawling through a combat zone, just waiting for the other boot to drop. But I am, sort of. There are snipers everywhere.

My friend's life had been the picture of the perfect family. She was a devoted wife and mother. He was a doctor. She was active in her church and tried to do everything right. Then, one Christmas, she was blindsided by the revelation that her husband had been cheating on her for years.

Now, you might think, How can someone be that blind? There had to have been red flags everywhere, right? Not necessarily. When you're a relatively trusting person dealing with a pathological liar, you can be taken in. The cheater divorced my friend and married the adulterous woman, who was apparently comfortable with obliterating a family. My friend was devastated, obviously, but she eventually began to heal. She married a great guy and her tribe of three kids increased to six.

This story had a happy ending, as many of these painful stories do. But the carnage that needed to be worked through first was brutal. I hear plenty of stories like this. They don't surprise me anymore, except for one part. What I never get used to hearing about is the "devoted father" who leaves his children and blissfully starts a new family. *Umm . . . hello! You have children!*

Then they become deacons in their new church and find all sorts of ways to distort 2 Corinthians 5:17: "Therefore, if anyone is in Christ, the new creation has come: The old has gone, the new is here!" *Really?*

My friend had been through the ringer, no doubt. Divorce can be worse than death, because at least in death there's no rejection. But she'd also done a lot of things right; three in particular:

1. She stayed connected to people who supported her, prayed for her, listened without judgment, and allowed her to cry until her face began to melt.

2. She had worked before starting a family and kept working, at least a few hours a week, while bringing up her kids. That way, when the time came, she was able to step back into a job she loved. (Good advice for empty nesters too.)

3. She refused to allow her bitterness to linger after the pain was processed. I believe this is what enabled her to love again.

Now life is good. So good, in fact, she feels like some of her friends are a little mad at her for being so happy. They remind me of a commercial I used to see on TV in the '80s. A beautiful model selling hair products would look into the camera and say, "Don't hate me because I'm beautiful." Whenever I saw that commercial, I remember thinking, I don't hate you. I find you incredibly annoying, but I don't hate you.

Jealously is a strange force of nature. My friend's friends would never have admitted it, but envy had crept into their frustrated midlives. Disappointed with the way things turned out with their kids, their husbands, or their careers left them ungracious, to say the least.

Searching for Solutions

No one really wants to be ungracious. Fortunately, there are more solutions for our discontentment than we think. They just get camouflaged by our slightly damaged emotions. But trust me, they're there. They're just waiting for us to discover them and breathe them in like fresh air.

When my son was five years old, my husband thought it was time for him to learn how to water ski. His sixth birthday was fast approaching and, according to my hubby, the boy was almost over the hill.

My husband had learned how to ski at his aunt's lake house when he was young. He'd mastered all types of skiing, including slaloming (his spray was phenomenal), kneeboarding (no wonder he needed them replaced), and barefooting (nature's not-so-gentle enema). Now, with big plans for his own son, I watched him fast becoming the poster child for overzealous parents.

One day, after launching his Spydercraft, he dove into the crisp bay water to tighten my son's skis. Both heads bobbled up and down as my husband gave last-minute instructions to a boy who looked as though he wished he were anywhere but behind that boat.

I was filming the big event when my husband yelled, "Hit it!" and like most new skiers, my son immediately wiped out. But for some reason, instead of letting go of the rope, he held on. Even as my cousin swung the boat around to retrieve him, he clung to the rope facedown, dragging through the water and nearly drowning himself.

We frantically yelled, "Let go of the rope!" and what felt like a lifetime later, my son, waterlogged and gasping for air, finally let go. This marked the beginning and the end of his skiing career, much to his father's chagrin. My husband tried his best to persuade our son to give it one more college try, but his words fell on deaf ears, and I told him to get a life.

Later that day, as I snuggled with my son on the couch, I asked him why he held on to the rope even after he'd fallen. He reminded me of a day we'd all gone sledding the winter before. When he was about to make his first run, my husband gave him one instruction, "Don't let go." And he didn't.

In fact, he held on so tightly that when he flew down the hill and hit a bump, he was literally catapulted into the air and did an amazing 360-degree flip before sticking the landing. He didn't know what hit him, but Shaun White would have been impressed. That's when I realized what had happened. Somehow the instructions for sledding got mixed up with the instructions for skiing, and my boy did not let go.

I think a lot of us are being dragged facedown and gasping for air. Some of us will give up too quickly and sell ourselves short. As Thomas Edison put it, "Many of life's failures are people who did not realize how close they were to success when they gave up."

That said, there are probably plenty of us who refuse to recognize when it is time to let go. Every coach and motivational speaker we've ever heard has told us, "Never give up. We can do anything we set our minds to." But that's simply not true. We can't do everything we set our minds to. No matter how much I may want to be a sought-after soloist, a brain surgeon, or a supermodel, it's not gonna happen. And trying to make it happen would only frustrate me and leave me disillusioned with life.

It's good to dream big and build on both failures and successes. We also need to figure out the things in life we can control and then control them. We might be surprised at how much control we actually have, which, to some extent, even includes the things we can't control, namely, how we respond to them.

A little soul-searching can point us in a new direction and show us that "plan B" may have been better suited for our success all along. Maybe it's time to let go of the rope and find the fresh air that's right there.

"See, I am doing a new thing! Now it springs up; do you not perceive it?" (Isaiah 43:19).

It's a Process

It's hard to cultivate contentment in a world that thrives on drama. Attention-grabbing headlines are the name of the game, which makes it hard to know what to believe. As we grow older, we tend to become more discerning of the "information overload." The goal is to sift through the hype and learn how to separate the stuff that builds us up from the stuff that tears us down, grow cautious without becoming cynical. Because, in case you didn't notice, the "experts" have pretty much declared all things pleasurable and adventuresome to be hazardous to our health.

It's hard to cultivate contentment in a world that thrives on drama.

Seriously, I realize none of us is getting out of this life alive, but is everything really that dangerous? All within the span of one week, I heard:

> French fries can kill us.
> Skinny jeans cause nerve damage.

Sitting shortens our lifespan.
Artificial sweeteners are making
  us fat.
Cell phones cause brain cancer.
Washing machines spread *E. coli.*
Brushing damages our tooth enamel.
Facebook causes depression.
Neckties raise blood pressure.
Exercise shrinks genitals.

Here's the problem. Not only have news programs become ravenous vultures looking to strip the meat off our unsuspecting bones but also the medical establishment has become big business too. Together they've become the bullies on the playground. We *want* to do the right thing, but they keep changing their minds about what the right thing is.

The kind of discernment that leads to contentment is a process. When I was a young mom trying to do the right thing, I was totally yanked around by the information the "experts" put out there. And now, with social media, things have gotten much worse.

I wanted to do everything right with my new baby and was just naive enough to be impressed by every new "study" that came along. I mean, if it was reported on *World News Tonight,* it had to be true, right? But as the years rolled by, I started noticing inconsistencies in the data depending on who was conducting the study. For instance, guidelines for healthy cholesterol are bound to be lower when the studies are conducted by companies that manufacture statins.

First, we were told caffeine would give us heart attacks. Then we were told it would prevent Alzheimer's.

If we wanted to lose weight, we were told to eat carbs and avoid fats. Then we learned carbs were making us fat, and fats would make us thin.

Margarine was supposed to be a better alternative to the saturated fat found in butter. Then we learned margarine contained trans fats and would clog our arteries even quicker.

Eggs were off-limits if you had high cholesterol. Then, somehow, they became a miracle food for everyone.

For years we were instructed to stay out of the sun. Next thing we knew, our sunscreen had carcinogens and our lack of vitamin D was lowering our immunity.

My mom's generation was told that hormone replacement therapy would prevent heart attacks, dementia, and bone loss. Ten years later, it caused all three.

I suspected a conspiracy, but it took me almost two decades to realize that fear tactics and bad journalism were to blame. News programs are about ratings, not necessarily the truth. I found myself getting really annoyed with journalists who were supposed to be giving both sides to every story. They should be fired—along with the guy whose idea it was to put glass walls in the newsroom. (Am I the only one irritated by the people waving furiously behind the anchors as they talk about war and famine?)

My insecurities as a new mom, combined with my panic disorder, made me ripe for fear. And trust me, it's hard to be content when you're afraid of every new danger and disease that comes your way. Facts get quickly blown out of proportion, and, in a weak moment, we fall for these false narratives. I don't know who said it first, but like all the other hypochondriacs in the world, I told my husband he might as well write on my tombstone, "I told you I was sick."

The warning from the last few summers about "dry drowning" (when children inhale enough water to inflame their lungs and inhibit their breathing hours after swimming) was the straw that broke the camel's back—and put it in traction for months. As I sat by the pool watching my nieces play, I thought, *Do parents really need one more thing to worry about?* The sun, the sunscreen, the chlorine, the pool filters, the snacks. What's left?

Lenore Skenazy, a journalist and mother of two, published a *Huffington Post* article in 2009 about letting her nine-year-old son take the subway by himself. Skenazy had been blogging about the unnecessary guilt and fear the media dump on moms today with inflated reports and exaggerated warnings. But after writing her article about the subway, which brought swift criticism and concerns of child abuse, Skenazy went viral. This led to her book *Free Range Kids: How to Raise Safe, Self-Reliant Children (Without Going*

Nuts with Worry) and earned her the nickname "World's Worst Mom," which became the title of her reality show.

When I first heard an interview with Skenazy in 2009, I didn't get the feeling she started any of this to get attention. Instead, the Yale grad was on a personal crusade to expose the skewed reporting that steals the joy of parenting and leads to bubble-wrapped children. Skenazy is definitely onto something. Neurotic parenting has gotten out of hand.

Recently I caught an old episode of *My Three Sons* that was filmed in 1960. It centered on the youngest son feeling left out because his older brothers, a middle schooler and a high schooler, were going camping without him. As I watched, I thought of how different things are today. A 2019 plotline wouldn't have centered on the boy feeling left out; rather, it would have targeted the father's neglect for letting his kids camp in the woods by themselves.

Is a news story like "dry drowning" really necessary? Obviously, we need to watch our kids at the pool. And yes, if they're having trouble breathing, they should be taken to the doctor. But "dry drownings" are extremely rare. In fact, an autopsy of the boy who purportedly died from "dry drowning" and triggered the scare in 2017 revealed that he actually died of a heart condition unrelated to drowning. But by then, the hysteria had begun.[2]

How much of our contentment are we willing to forfeit by worrying about something that may never happen?

Now let's look at another frightening threat: child abduction. According to David Finkelhor, Director of the Crimes Against Children Research Center at the University of New Hampshire, only one-hundredth of one percent of all missing children are taken by strangers. Yet, gone are the days when kids actually rode their bikes to the park.

Now, I realize, if your child is the one-hundredth of one percent, it's a tragedy. It's quite a different story. But the question is, how much of our contentment are we willing to forfeit by worrying about something that may never happen? Far greater is the danger of letting social media and a fertile imagination make our kids high-strung and fearful.

Skenazy's book spoke to me because I've had a hard time learning that worrying changes nothing. *NOTHING, I tells ya!* Well, maybe one thing. It does chip away at our sense of contentment.

So, if you're a worrier, it may be time to find a new hobby, one that doesn't take such a toll on your mind and your body. I suggest the timeless art of "doing your best and leaving God with the rest."

Maybe it's worth looking into the wise instruction given to us thousands of years ago by the third king of Israel. His words are a saving grace for those of us who'd prefer a bubble-wrapped world. "Trust in the LORD with all your heart and lean not on your own understanding; in all your ways submit to him, and he will make your paths straight" (Proverbs 3:5-6).

Chapter Three

WHAT ARE YOU WAITING FOR?

Discontented people may need to ask themselves a few questions, beginning with, What am I *really* looking for? What would bring me joy? Not the pleasure-bursts of happiness that come from a chocolate chip cookie fresh from the oven or a kiss from the guy you've been waiting for. Both may be yummy in their own way, but if we're looking for something more substantial, something that can weather the inevitable highs and lows of life, we may need to expand our search just a bit.

I've discovered that even the good things in life can be dangerous if we hang all our hopes on them. If the only things we've invested ourselves in are our looks or careers or our kids, what happens when those things are taken away? That's right. Kids are *supposed* to leave you, though no one cleared that plan with me.

The toughest part about reaching middle age was being fired from a job I put everything into. For more than twenty years I was a stay-at-home mom, and I loved it. As far as I'm concerned, women's liberation is about choice, and I was fortunate enough to be the mom I wanted to be. My husband was the breadwinner, which allowed me to run the household and do my nonprofit work on the side. But my plans beyond that were sketchy. In fact, I remember the day I sensed trouble looming.

I was sitting at a women's event listening to a speaker talk about her painful empty nest experience. My kids were only toddlers at the time, but that didn't stop the cold chill from slicing through me as I contemplated the impending loneliness.

Since grieving things in advance has always been my style, right then and there I should have committed to having more babies. Lots of babies, even if it meant one day they'd probably have to commit me.

I've always loved the idea of a big family: three boys and three girls. Though as with all good fantasies I tended to gloss over the hard work of a huge tribe. I guess I sort of pictured them perpetually at camp . . . returning to me when they were ready to rise up and call me blessed. That's why I can't be trusted to counsel women who are wondering whether they should have another baby. They shouldn't ask for my opinion, especially if they don't *really* want more kids. I'm definitely skewed toward "the more the merrier."

Back then, I figured the nonprofit work I did would be enough to distract me when my kids grew up. It wasn't high paying, but it was rewarding and time consuming, and I was sure it would help fill the void I sensed hurtling my way.

And it should have. But instead of finding ways to expand my work when my nest was empty, the grief I felt caused me to turn inward, and I isolated myself in many different ways. Sadness prefers solitude, but I wouldn't recommend it.

Sadness prefers solitude, but I wouldn't recommend it.

Times were changing, though, and no matter how much I loved baking cupcakes and being room mother, much like everything else, my role in their lives was being downsized. And there was nothing I could do to stop it. It didn't matter that I wasn't ready to give up parent/teacher conferences, field trips, and sporting events. It didn't matter that I still enjoyed buying school supplies, making beds, and organizing lunches. I was clearly being edged out of my position, and it was truly painful.

I'm lucky, though. Sensing my pain, my grown kids have generously offered to let me make their beds and lunches whenever the urge strikes.

Change is hard, especially when you liked the way things were. I guess in that sense the pain could be a gift. It's evidence of a happy time. However, transitioning from a hands-on coach to a sidelined cheerleader was hard for me. I didn't feel much like celebrating.

Let's face it, we get used to bossing our kids around and telling them what to wear, what to eat, and when to go to bed. The control is intoxicating. And loosening our white-knuckled grip on their lives isn't easy. Our instincts are to protect and provide. And the timing isn't great either, because right about the time we've gained some serious insights, our kids are unimpressed. They prefer to learn things for themselves, which is exactly what worries us. It can be hard to watch. We're warned not to live vicariously through our children, but without serious sedation, how is that possible? We celebrate our kid's homerun as though *we* had just hit it out of the park. We suffer their rejection as though *we* were left without a prom date.

But here's the problem. When we think that a person, *any* person, is put on the planet to fulfill our needs, we set ourselves up for major disappointment. We also put unreasonable demands on them. As my grandma used to say, "Heaven help the daughter whose mother never made the squad."

Transitions can be painful. Broken marriages, lost jobs, and empty nests can feel like death if those are the things that complete us. I remember the day my daughter handed me my pink slip and said, "Mom, I need you to stop being my teacher and just be my friend."

It was time to find another occupation.

Problem People

Difficult people are a major source of discontentment. We were made for relationships. That much is true. But what catches us off guard is when we put everything into a relationship and it still gets messed up. It's even tougher when bowing out of that relationship isn't an easy option, as with family members or coworkers.

I never had strained relationships with my parents or siblings, so I was completely caught off guard when I started struggling with my teenage daughter. I didn't realize it at the time, but I obviously had all sorts of preconceived notions of what she was "supposed" to be. Consequently, I had lots of painful moments when I thought parenthood was seriously overrated. Then one day I heard a family counselor say that parenthood, at best, is delayed gratification. This put a new spin on things for me. Our kids aren't here to entertain us or meet our needs. They're on loan, so to speak, and the goal is to find ways we can all learn and grow together.

This perspective helped me hang in there through my daughter's difficult years when giving up was not an option. She'd always been the feisty one, but when the hormones of midlife came crashing into the hormones of adolescence, our home felt like a train wreck. And if Mrs. Bateman's eighth grade science class taught me anything, it's that some elements are dangerous when mixed.

Many nights I lamented to my husband, "Wasn't the Virgin Mary out of the house by fifteen?" My daughter had been full of joy and creativity until the seventh grade. Then we moved from Milwaukee to Chicago, and all that creative energy turned into anger. The transition to a new middle school was difficult. The kids were different. She still loved Disney movies and Sailor Moon, but her new classmates were all about makeup and boyfriends.

It took me a while to recognize that her anger toward me was, in fact, pain she didn't know how to process. She couldn't label it, but she showed it in a million ways. That's what difficult people do. Every conversation was strained, and I longed for the phase I'd been warned about as a young mom when a teen starts lying to his or her parents and telling them everything they want to hear. But that phase never came. In fact, I don't remember hearing anything from her I wanted to hear for about five years.

And I drove her crazy too. My interest was invasive, my concern was irritating, my advice was intrusive. I couldn't say anything—good or bad—without it turning into a fight.

Even her humor was hurtful toward me, like the time I walked into the living room wearing a brand-new outfit. She looked me up and down and asked, "Are you wearing *that*?"

I told her no, I was just stretching it out.

But time moves quickly, even with difficult people, and I remember thinking I'd better find some teenage moments to savor before they completely vanished. Though sometimes that took some serious searching.

I noticed myself feeling angry with God too. This wasn't what I'd signed up for. I wanted to enjoy my daughter. I worked very hard to be a good mom. I had followed the rules. But somewhere along the line I began to realize something. Certainly, my daughter had her share of painful disappointments, bad breaks, and bad choices. But I wondered if her failures were being blown out of proportion like some crazy funhouse mirror.

I had become a dry sponge, absorbing every drop of her disappointment, and it often left me feeling worse than she did. But now, on the other side of her teen years, I can see the big picture. And in many ways, she did better than I thought.

She also taught me a thing or two in the process, such as how to pray. I thought I knew, but I really didn't. She taught me to trust God's control too by generously giving me daily reminders of how little I had. *Thank you, darling.*

And if I was ever tempted to be judgmental, she cured me of that as well. It's a funny thing about passing judgment, because we don't see ourselves as snobs. But how often do we look at people and determine their value based on education, ethnicity, sexuality, or number of tattoos? Do we see their hardships and assume they could have done something to avoid them? I had thought I was more evolved than that. Still, before my daughter turned sixteen, I was pretty sure nose piercings and citations for underage drinking were reserved for kids who came from troubled homes. Clearly, their parents were disengaged in some way.

Wrong again.

I remember visiting with a fellow hockey mom when my daughter was a sweet seven-year-old. As we watched my daughter skip by happily, smiling at me, my friend turned to me and said, "Just wait till she's sixteen and doesn't want to be seen with you."

> I started to surround myself with people who had actually been there—people who actually understood it.

Her comment surprised me, and I honestly remember thinking, *No way, lady. That'll never happen to me.* My friend struggled with her daughter because she had family issues. I, on the other hand, came from an intact family and was deeply in touch with myself and my child.

Looking back, it's kind of crazy that I believed this would never happen to me. In fact, I'm always surprised when I see people interviewed on the news after some tragedy. They always say, "I never thought this could happen to me." But I just assume I'll be the first to look at the camera and say, "I knew this was going to happen."

Ten years later, I was on my knees sobbing about my daughter. I threw everything I had at God, which was good because He's God, and He can handle it. But I remember the moment distinctly because I had an epiphany almost as clear as an audible voice. As I begged God to take the problems away, He said, "Lean in, baby. This isn't going to be over anytime soon, but I'll walk you through it."

It may sound strange, but I looked at things differently after that. Why should I expect my sixteen-year-old to have the wisdom of a twenty-six-year-old—the age when I started to get a clue? That day, I heeded the warning and began making a conscious effort to gird my loins, so to speak, and build a support system. I started to surround myself with people who had actually been there—people who actually understood it.

Rolling in the Mud

Clearly, contentment can feel like an uphill battle. But that's okay, as long as we remain a "work in progress." Happiness experts, such as Tal Ben-Shahar from Harvard University, have looked at the research and discovered the importance of validating our pain. There are no shortcuts, and if we think we've arrived, we probably haven't, which is something I was reminded of not long after my short-sale saga.

One morning, two moms were sitting at my kitchen table asking me to pray for their grown daughters. But honestly, I wasn't feeling it. For weeks I'd been indulging in negative thoughts and wondered if they should be asking someone else to pray for their kids—someone more up for the task.

To my right was a mom hoping for some sort of sign that her daughter was still alive. She hadn't heard from her in weeks. As she wiped her eyes with a wad of tissues, she said, "She's lost her apartment. She's lost her job. She's lost her phone." The woman wondered who might find her daughter first. The police? A supplier? Most of her daughter's friends had failed rehab too, so there was no one she could call.

As I watched her struggle with her words, I was reminded of all the overwhelmed moms I'd met through the years. Through their guilt and shame, they'd confess to me how sometimes, late at night, when the pain makes sleeping impossible, they wished God would take their child. Then, at least, they'd know where that child was.

To my left was another mom also asking for prayer. Her daughter was trying to choose among three top universities that had already sent her letters of interest. She also needed to decide on a major, which was tricky because she was proficient in both math and science.

I was afraid to speak, so I sat at my table taking it all in. I could feel the rumbling deep inside of me. It was like distant thunder from a storm I'd been tracking for weeks. I knew it was about to break, but I'd done nothing to prepare for it. Life was so unfair. How could I be expected to pray for this mess? I could sort of understand bad things happening to bad people, but how could God treat His own this way? I felt the fingers of bitterness tightening around my neck.

If the woman on my left could "praise Jesus" for the

enormous house she lived in, her two gifted children, and her devoted CEO husband—shouldn't the woman on my right be able to blame Him for the husband who abandoned her and left their three kids reeling?

Obviously, I was struggling.

Fortunately, our time together ended before my storm made landfall. The bitterness clung to me, though, throughout the morning and even as I drove to the post office that afternoon. As I stood in the interminably long line, I had plenty of time to think about all that was wrong with the world: racism, greed, poverty, war.

As my list of grievances grew, everything annoyed me, including the blonde lady standing toward the front of the line. Her smile was a contrast to everything I felt inside. She was too perky with her tight little body and smooth young face. She probably lived in the beautiful subdivision I used to live in back when I was perky. That was before mortgages were handed out like candy that all too soon turned to septic waste. She was probably on her way to pick up her kids from soccer practice and cheerleading. I imagined them chatting easily in their shiny black Suburban as they discussed who they'd let take them to the dance.

As I stood there shifting my weight from side to side, I wondered if this was how people actually went postal. Too many thoughts in a confined space with too much time to think. But then another thought hit me. A really disturbing one. Maybe the lady with the nice face who smiled at everyone didn't even have kids. Maybe her skinny jeans fit because she had just finished her last round of chemo. Maybe those blonde locks were a gift from Wigs by Vanessa to cover the traces of treatment.

Ugh. Why couldn't I just complain to God without feeling guilty? Why couldn't my faulty perspective of Him linger for just a little while longer? Now I was really annoyed and thought about quitting prayer altogether. I was tired of being pushed into places I didn't want to go. Sometimes I didn't feel like being grateful or content. I wanted to savor my discontentment and roll around with it in the mud, and prayer had a way of hosing me down.

Discomfort Zone

In my messiest moments, I've wondered, is it *really* better to have loved and lost than never to have loved at all? Tennyson seemed to think so. But sometimes I'm not so sure. I suppose the poet's words ring true when all is well with our world: when our lives are in balance, our relationships are strong, and the bills are paid. But when we suffer a great loss, that little adage sounds like crazy talk. Suddenly, it makes more sense to say, "If I'd never had what I just lost, I wouldn't know what I'm missing now."

When my daughter was about four years old, she had a mysterious aversion to balloons. We'd visit carnivals and parades and see lots of kids with colorful balloons tied to their wrists or strollers. But whenever I offered her one, she'd shake her little head and say, "No thank you." She never explained why, and she never wavered. So, I tried my best to figure it out.

I noticed she didn't mind the smaller balloons, the ones you risk passing out from when you inflate them yourself. And she definitely liked water balloons that turned her into a little assassin on a hot day. But the pretty balloons, the ones filled with helium that are irresistible to most kids, she found very resistible.

Finally, the truth came out when she reminded me of a balloon that got away. I'd forgotten how the wind took it higher and higher as she stood powerless to retrieve it. She was devastated and had no intention of risking it again.

Loss is painful, and I'm a big believer in validating that pain. There's nothing quite like a good pity party, especially when you invite the right guests and throw the best confetti. But as with all good parties, pity can't last forever.

Life is full of risks that involve pain and loss. But if we play it safe and say "no thank you" to every balloon we're offered, things can get fairly bland. And I speak from experience. When my thirteen-year panic disorder was finally diagnosed and treated as an adrenaline issue, I was content just to live. I took very few risks because life was good in my little cocoon. I had no intention of rocking the boat. But as the years raced by, I started counting the cost of risk-free living. I began to think about all the things I might be missing.

That's when I knew it was time to take a few chances again. So, as crazy as it sounded, I decided to try my hand as a writer and a speaker.

I've often said that pitching a manuscript to a publisher is not unlike standing naked in front of a group of strangers and asking, "What do you think?" I knew the risk of rejection, but my boredom and my lack of productivity began to outweigh my fear of failure. That's when I knew it was time for a change.

We're wired to take risks, to fail, and to try again.

I did exactly what I tell others to do: I began with a few baby steps, because the lower the risk, the easier the fall. My writing goals began small . . . a little freelancing here, a few writers' conferences there. How hard could it be to ask editors to evaluate your work anonymously? Who cares if they pan it when you'll never see them again? So, I plowed forward, and before I knew it, I was picked up by a publisher and became an author.

Life is about creating, exploring, and evolving. We're wired to take risks, to fail, and to try again. The balloons are just waiting, and, basically, we only have two choices. We can play it safe and never take a chance. That way we're sure never to fail. Or we can get out there and say, "What the heck. I'm tired of waiting!"

But let's not be stupid about it. Self-awareness is an important tool when you're taking risks. I knew my skin wasn't as thick as it should be for a burgeoning writer (not that thin skin is always a bad thing). I have a ginormous capacity for empathy, and much of it comes from being wounded myself. I just have to keep that in mind and create a plan that makes space for potential meltdowns. I began the process of having my writing critiqued by people who would temper their criticism with kindness. I needed them to be honest without destroying me. That's how confidence is built, one small step and one small victory at a time.

And, clearly, my entire writing experience made me realize how underrated discontentment can be. Not that rejection is an easy thing. Definitely not. But discontentment can keep us from getting *too* comfortable. It can push us to explore, expand, and grow in areas we'd never take the time to if life was always peachy. We're wired to take chances, and we need to learn how to fail successfully.

Martha Snell Nicholson was born in 1898 and lived in Washington State. Most of her adult life was plagued by illnesses, including debilitating arthritis that kept her bedridden until she died in 1953. But instead of allowing her bitterness to crush her, she channeled all her pain into her writing and became a poet. She used her lack of mobility to contemplate life and invite God to strengthen her spirit.

I'm not a very poetic person, but she penned one of my favorite poems that can bring me to tears every time I read it. It's a masterpiece, as far as I'm concerned. It's called "Treasures."

One by one He took them from me,
All the things I valued most,
Until I was empty-handed;
Every glittering toy was lost.
And I walked earth's highways, grieving.
In my rags and poverty.
Till I heard His voice inviting,
"Lift your empty hands to Me!"
So I held my hands toward heaven,
And He filled them with a store
Of His own transcendent riches,
Till they could contain no more.
And at last I comprehended
With my stupid mind and dull,
That God could not pour His riches
Into hands already full!

The way the poet confronts her disappointments and then invites God to meet her needs totally amazes me. I'd like to think I could be a Martha Snell Nicholson. But given the same set of circumstances, I can't be sure. It's always hard to imagine being in someone else's shoes because God rarely gives us grace to worry about "potential" adversity or someone else's struggle. He's more about supplying grace as needed. And, here again, I speak from experience.

It should bring us enormous comfort to know God will supply what we need when we need it. Whether through a friend, an encouraging word, or a completely altered set of circumstances, we can rest on this assurance. Which is good, because in case you didn't notice, this life can get really hard.

Enough Potential

I'm always inspired by stories of people who didn't listen to the negative talk. Back in school, author John Irving was a mediocre student and labeled lazy and stupid. It wasn't until his brother Brendan was diagnosed with dyslexia that he realized he had the same condition. The diagnosis turned his life around, and he went on to become the best-selling author of *The World According to Garp* and *The Cider House Rules*.

In *The Genius in All of Us*, David Shenk points out that a hundred years ago, when primary school became mandatory in France, the Intelligence Quotient (IQ) test was developed to help educators identify where students should be placed in terms of educational needs. Since then, the IQ test has helped screen military recruits and identify individuals' strengths for suitable job placement. But it's had its harmful effects too. Immigrants entering Ellis Island were viewed as less intelligent when they scored poorly on the test, which, by the way, was administered in English. The Nazis even used the test to identify the "undesirables" in their attempt at ethnic cleansing.

Professor Jordan B. Peterson from the University of Toronto explains how, after extensive research, the IQ test remains our best screening tool, although, like Shenk, he sees how unreliable it can be. People who have been reared in a nurturing environment tend to score higher. Shenk points out that it would be much more telling if we could create a diagnostic tool that measures potential rather than what a person has been exposed to.

The truth is, we're all the product of many factors, including our genetics, our personality traits, the choices we make, and the environment we were brought up in. I discovered all of this for myself years ago. My life had been one big social event until my third year of college. Up to that point, I'd never thought of myself as a good student because my grades were average at best . . . never mind the fact that I never studied. Cheerleading, boys, happy hour. What else was there? I even managed to get through my entire first year at the university without ever stepping foot inside the campus library. And this was before the internet.

How I was able to graduate in four years remains a mystery to me, though it may have had something to do with the "pep talk" my dad gave me. After seeing the grades I'd gotten in some of the Gen Ed classes I kept blowing off, he calmly said, "If I see another D, I'm done paying."

That was that.

But the entire party ended abruptly anyway when a mysterious panic disorder rocked my world. Fueled by the adrenaline of an undiagnosed heart condition, my life became painfully serious, and I was plagued by questions about life and God. I needed answers for everything, and I couldn't find them fast enough. I surrounded myself with books and knew how to find every bookstore and every library in every city. In fact, the questions began to roll through me so forcefully, it was as if I'd never really thought about anything before.

Ironically, during my struggle, my grades improved. I guess pain can be a great motivator.

Thirteen years later, when I was finally diagnosed and treated, my relief was overwhelming. But I had to "unlearn" some things about myself I'd come to believe. For one thing, I was stronger and smarter than I thought. Most of us are.

My panic disorder had already kept me from doing lots of things I was interested in, such as traveling more, expanding my education, and having more kids. But I didn't want to waste any more time living in regret, even though I'd come up with dozens of creative ways to do so. Instead, I decided to make up for lost time as a writer and a very unlikely public speaker. I am passionate about reminding people that if you still have a pulse, it's never too late. Undiagnosed learning problems, emotional disorders, or dysfunctional upbringings—in the end, it doesn't really matter.

It's never too late to discover what we're capable of.

From Benjamin Franklin to Grandma Moses, we're taught it's never too late to discover what we're capable of. Singing, dancing, writing, painting—we need to let our genius out and boost our sense of well-being.

Facing Discouragement

Kate Bowler is in her thirties. She's a wife, a mom, and a professor at Duke Divinity School. She is also fighting cancer. I've never met her, but she fast became my new BFF the moment I read her *New York Times* article, "Death, the Prosperity Gospel, and Me." I felt a connection to her immediately.

She'd just completed a book called *Blessed: A History of the American Prosperity Doctrine* in which she examines the connection between suffering and faith. As an author who's written on the topic of doubt, I too have done my homework in this area. I needed to know why we struggle with doubt and disillusionment and what we can do about it.

I grew up in an evangelical home where love reigned supreme and where all my needs were met. I've never been abused, discriminated against, or lived as a refugee. My parents were never devotees of the prosperity doctrine or any other "Holy Ghost" movement. But as a student of history, I've seen over the past hundred years or so how this "health and wealth" doctrine has seeped into our cultural consciousness on every level. For many, it's left a painful disconnect between the God of the Bible and a culture that's hijacked the message of Christ. We're no longer made in the image of God. We've made Him into ours.

Bowler says, "The prosperity gospel popularized a Christian explanation for why some people make it and some do not. They revolutionized prayer as an instrument for getting

God always to say 'yes.' Follow these rules, and God will reward you, heal you, restore you."[1]

And the illusion of control is held on to until the very end, Bowler explains. "If a believer gets sick and dies, shame compounds the grief. Those who are loved and lost are just that—those who have lost the test of faith."

This kind of discouragement is the recipe for disillusionment and discontentment. We all need a framework or a language we can use to make sense of suffering. Even before Kate Bowler was given her devastating diagnosis, as a biblical scholar, she knew there is no promise for perfection this side of eternity. She reminds us that while God offers a substantial kind of healing, it won't be complete until we are in His presence. The apostle Paul said it this way: "Though outwardly we are wasting away, yet inwardly we are being renewed day by day" (2 Corinthians 4:16).

When I think about suffering in the world, I can't "defend" God or His actions. But more to the point, He hasn't asked me to. Instead, He's shown me that the high cost of "freedom of choice" brings with it the chance that things can get messed up. But it's in the black backdrop of despair that He's also shown me how His grace can shine at its brightest—not the delusional type of encouragement that comes from self-deception, but something much, much deeper that reaches beyond anything this sorry girl could conjure up.

When asked how her prayer life had changed in the months since her diagnosis, Kate Bowler said, "Prayer has become radical dependence on the assumption that God will be there no matter what. It's just been a radical revelation of His presence."

My new BFF makes good sense to me. She knows that adversity can be difficult and clarifying at the same time. She also knows that sometimes it's impossible to see God without it.

Foxhole Prayers

It's hard to see the good side of the bad things, but there is one. That's what redemption is all about. Those difficult moments remind us of our need for a higher power to come and redeem our pain and make those moments useful.

They remind us to pray, and in the process, our priorities have a way of shifting. Our hearts and minds become transformed through our serious petition, as the apostle Paul points out in the Book of Philippians. Though, sometimes, our prayers are reduced to the "foxhole" variety, which I'm not knocking. All prayer is important.

When I was in high school, I saw this offbeat comedy at the drive-in. It was called *The End*, and it starred Burt Reynolds and his real-life best friend Dom DeLuise. It was the ultimate example of desperate foxhole prayer.

Sonny, Reynold's character, was told he didn't have long to live, so he tried to commit suicide. But when his botched attempt landed him in the psych ward, he met another patient named Marlon, played by DeLuise. Marlon was a simple-minded, loveable guy who was committed to helping his new friend kill himself. But nothing Marlon tried seemed to work.

What I remember most about the movie was how it ended, which was both hilarious and insightful. After Marlon's failed attempts, Sonny finally decided to take matters into his own hands and swim out into the ocean. But when he got as far as he could reach, he had a sudden change of heart and decided he didn't want to drown. Realizing how far he was from shore, Sonny frantically called out to God for help and began promising Him everything. "I'll be a better father! I'll be a better person! Please, Lord, just make me a better swimmer!"

Sonny promised God everything he could think of. He would try to keep the Ten Commandments, though after struggling to recite them he promised to learn them first. He promised to be honest in business and not sell lakeside lots unless there actually was a lake around. He promised to give God 50 percent of his money, pointing out that no one does that. "We're talking *gross*, Lord!" he yelled, sucking air and trying not to sink. But the closer Sonny got to shore, the more the percentage of his giving began to shrink. It was quickly down to 10 percent, and by the time he reached shore, it was pretty evident all bets were off.

The movie ended with Sonny collapsing with relief on the shore. But crazy Marlon, unaware of Sonny's change of heart, was waiting behind the rocks with a butcher knife. The fiercely devoted friend was unwilling to believe Sonny had changed his mind, and the movie ended with Sonny running for his life and making new promises to God.

Most of us don't wear the look of desperation and disillusionment very well.

I've always thought *The End* was a great example of our typical attitude toward God. When things are going smoothly, we're fine with keeping Him at a distance. We love Him, or at least believe He is there, in theory. But when things get difficult, we wonder where the heck He is. Are you there, God? Do you even care?

I'm not quite Sonny, flailing around in the ocean and yelling at God. Not today, anyway. But I'm not quite the apostle Paul either (a slightly better role model).

When Paul wrote his letter to the church in Corinth (1 Corinthians 12) and told them about a struggle he'd been facing, he admitted how he felt like he was drowning too. He had begged God to remove his affliction, but God told him He had another plan. Not the lack of a plan, but another plan, which was to perfect His strength amid Paul's weakness. In the process, Paul gained an entirely new perspective.

Perspective

Contentment has a lot to do with our perspective. And pain has a way of muddying up the water. When we're hurting, it's hard to see the whole picture, like the man who walked into his doctor's office complaining that his entire body hurt. The doctor told him to touch his head.

"Does that hurt?" the doctor asked him.

"Yes," the man answered.

The doctor said, "Touch your shoulder. Does that hurt?"

"Yes," the man said.

The two continued all the way down until the man touched his foot. The doctor asked, "Does that hurt?"

"Yes!" the man replied. "It hurts everywhere I touch."

"Well," the doctor said. "That makes sense. You have a dislocated finger."

Sometimes we need to take a giant step backward before we can move forward. We are creatures of habit and we close our minds in ways we're not even aware of.

I thought about this recently as I listened to a lecture on ancient Greece. I could picture the apostle Paul, the former Saul of Tarsus, standing on the Acropolis in Athens two thousand years ago. If he had told the listeners of his day that, one day, a man would be able to stand where they were standing and speak to men on the other side of the world, face-to-face, they would have called him a lunatic. *"Impossible! Illogical! We don't believe in miracles."*

Actually, the men whom Paul addressed in Athens were the sophisticated minds of their day. Yet they would have been unable to comprehend something like Skype, which was developed by two Scandinavian men and then purchased by Microsoft in 2011. Although Skype is useful and quite inventive, it's hardly a miracle. But it makes me wonder how many other things we might be missing purely because our minds won't budge.

Most of us don't wear the look of desperation and disillusionment very well. So, when our perspective gets all muddled up, we need to return to the place where clarity brings relief. And prayer can take us there.

Chapter Four

HEAD GAMES

Contentment is a head game. I'm reminded of that every time I go on a diet. If I'm busy, I can go hours without eating, especially when I'm trying to meet my editor's deadline. Then, at about three in the afternoon, I hit the wall. My eyes glaze over, and I'm not sure what I'm writing anymore. *Contentment is alll abouttt mmadjisnisrtbgovamxc . . . zzzzz* . . . But the moment I declare myself to be on a diet, I must eat. I become a crazed woman, like Chris Farley's SNL Gap Girl character Cindy reaching for some French fries. In his cute skirt and his exorcist voice, he says, *"Lay off me. I'm starrrving."*

It's amazing how the very same food that's been sitting on my shelf untouched for weeks suddenly becomes all I can think about. The stale chips, the soggy cookies . . . they're calling my name.

My most successful diets are the ones I've refused to call a diet. Like my 80/20 plan where I eat healthy Monday through Friday and tell myself I can go nuts on the weekends. And for some reason, just knowing I *can* go nuts makes me want to less. Head games!

It's all about perspective. Years ago, I heard a story that remains one of my favorites even today. It's about a man who was shipwrecked on a deserted island. He was desperate and alone. He spent his days struggling to survive, searching for food, and gathering branches to build himself shelter. At night, he'd collapse in exhaustion by the small fire he was finally able to start and pray God would rescue him. But months went by.

One day, still clinging to hope, the man left his shelter to find food. But when he returned, everything he'd struggled to build was engulfed in flames. His eyes burned as he watched the billows of smoke.

Dropping to his knees, he wept, "God! How could you let this happen when I begged you for help?" With his energy spent, he fell into a deep sleep and was awakened the next morning by the sound of voices on the beach. He looked up and saw a man dressed in a captain's uniform with several men standing behind him.

The shipwrecked man sobbed with joy and asked, "How did you find me?"

The captain answered, "We saw the smoke signals you sent up."

It's all about perspective and how you choose to see something.

I once watched a debate between two very brilliant men. William Lane Craig is an analytical philosopher and Christopher Hitchens was a journalist. Both men, brilliant thinkers, saw life so differently, as Craig is a believer and Hitchens was not.

Craig looked at the cosmos and saw evidence of God's fine-tuning, His design, and beauty. Hitchens looked at the same cosmos and saw the destruction of shooting stars, collapsed suns, and failed galaxies.

Changing our behaviors begins by changing our thoughts.

Craig saw evidence of God's grace and restoration amid mankind's faulty choices. Hitchens said that if there were a creator, he would appear to be capricious, cruel, and incompetent.

How does this happen? How can two people look at the same evidence and come to such different conclusions? And how were those different perspectives shaped? Personality? experience? choice?

A change of perspective is only possible when we understand why we see things the way we do. And this takes a certain amount of self-awareness. It's the crucial first step.

Stuck in a Rut

My bloodhound used to salivate every night when I locked the front door. There was nothing particularly tasty about our deadbolt, but Pavlov was right. Boone got a vanilla Oreo every night before I went up to bed, and he never let me forget it.

Most of us sweat the small stuff more than the big stuff without even being aware of it.

We're all creatures of habit, so it's easy to get stuck in a rut. But what separates us from animals is our ability to choose how we want to live. And changing our behaviors begins by changing our thoughts. It's all about exchanging old ones for new ones and keeping our goal clearly in mind, like Boone. This is how we become different people. It starts with our perspective.

There are two women in my life who inspire me with their perspective. Both had huge obstacles thrust their way three decades ago. Each was in her twenties when she contracted a serious illness, and though they have the right to complain, neither one seems to do much of it.

One was studying abroad when she got sick. As she dragged herself through the streets of London struggling to keep up with her classmates, she soon discovered she had type 1 diabetes. The other was diagnosed with rheumatoid arthritis after she stood up from the couch and her legs wouldn't work.

Both women are greeted by limitations every morning. And while most of us are busy complaining about pulled muscles, bad haircuts, or high gas prices, they seem to measure out their complaints judiciously. It's as though they make a conscious decision about which complaint is worth their time and effort.

Both could be really ticked off at God, too, and incredibly discontent. But, instead, they've learned the power of perspective. They seem to know that God sees their smoke signals and sends rescue ships, daily.

God Shows Up

The strange thing is, most of us sweat the small stuff more than the big stuff without even being aware of it. It's like a mosquito buzzing around our ear. Totally annoying, but we can't put our finger on it. We're actually built to face obstacles; we just don't know it. Or we don't want to know it. And, fortunately, most of us will never have to find out. But if we do, it's nice to know that there's Someone who offers to walk us through it.

I heard a bizarre story years ago that proved this. It sounded more like an urban legend than anything else. It involved kidnapping, drug trafficking, and a bizarre occult practice that resulted in human sacrifice. It sounded so bizarre, in fact, that I almost didn't listen. But news programs have a way of sucking us in, and they thrive on bizarre rarities. And here's the clincher: not only did I discover that the story was true, but it actually happened to a distant relative of mine.

He was a premed student from the University of Texas traveling to South Padre Island for spring break. Along with his fraternity brothers, and thousands of other college students, he parked his car and made the short trip across the border into Mexico where the drinking age was lower.

On the first evening of their trip, the friends drank beer, met girls, then headed safely back to their room at the Sheraton. On the second evening, the four fraternity brothers started back on foot over the bridge to where their car was parked. Two of them continued walking, but the other two stopped so that one of them could step into an alley and do what a guy needs to do after an evening of drinking. But when the young man stepped back onto the street, his friend had vanished.

The frantic fraternity brothers contacted the police, which set off a massive manhunt on both sides of the border. It took almost a month to find the body of Mark J. Kilroy, which, according to the *Brownsville Herald*, had been "tortured, dismembered, and offered up as human sacrifice in the twisted imaginings of drug traffickers, who thought that sacrifice offered them protection from detection."[1] The grisly crime scene uncovered more than a dozen dead bodies. They'd been used by drug dealers whose religious activities combined elements of voodoo, Satanism, and a bloody Aztec ritual called "santismo."

The details of the story were unsettling enough, but when I discovered it happened to a distant relative of mine (Mark's grandpa and my grandpa were brothers), the story became stranger still. And I wondered, *How does a family ever recover from something like that?*

Clearly, most of us will never come close to experiencing anything like this. The only reason I share this bizarre story is because it reminds us that when tragedy strikes, we basically have two options. We can lean into God or we can turn away.

Honestly, I've done plenty of both, and I can tell you from experience which one is better. The heartbroken parents chose to lean into God, too, where the "peace . . . which transcends all understanding" can be found (Philippians 4:7). That's how their healing began. They chose to hold tightly to their faith. So, by the time their son's body was discovered, they said they were relieved to find closure in the knowledge that he was safely in the presence of the Lord.

This gave them permission to find joy again and turn their pain into a passion for helping others. They eventually met with Congress and the President to set up a foundation that helps kids keep busy, safe, and productive, particularly during the summer months.

Fear

Fearing the worst is a waste of time. It chips away at our ability to fully engage in life and enjoy it. It's a contentment killer, and like any living thing, it needs fuel to survive. So, what are we feeding on? What are we looking at? Who are we listening to?

In the darkest days of my panic disorder, my life was fear on overdrive. Everything frightened me, and it became difficult to process things accurately. Some of the fears seem comical now, but trust me, there was nothing funny about them at the time.

Years ago, while driving through Baltimore on a particularly bad day, my shaky hands gripping the wheel, a guy on the radio said something about headhunters in the DC area. With virtually no business experience at the time, naturally I braced for the worst.

When Chicago was gifted a rare 80-degree day in March, I should have been enjoying it in my backyard. Instead, I was sure it signaled something cataclysmic like the end of the world.

I was so easily frightened in those days, I panicked over everything. I second-guessed my decisions and obsessed over conversations. I became a checker of locks, burners, moles, and bumps. I tightened my kids' car seats until their fingers turned blue.

Obviously, I was no fan of flying either. Even today, some of the fears that got deeply embedded still linger. But now I see those fears for what they are. When I became a speaker, I was called on to travel—a lot. While white-knuckling it through some turbulence on one flight, I was suddenly struck by the painful irony of being on my way to teach women how to trust God.

The pilot made an announcement over the intercom that none of us could hear and no one paid attention to. I was sure he was giving us our final instructions before the plane crashed. I grabbed the arm of the guy next to me and said, "I can't hear him. What's he saying?"

The guy looked at me and said, "Relax, lady. We're flying over the Rockies, and he wants us to enjoy the view."

I smiled with embarrassment and prayed he wouldn't ask what work I was in.

I knew I'd need to rein in this thing called fear. Even my daughter, who was about eight at the time, felt it necessary to comfort her mom as I gripped the armrests on another bumpy flight. As we neared the airport and spotted the lights of the runway, she began singing in my ear the *Mary Tyler Moore* song she'd learned from Nick at Nite. "You're gonna make it after all."

At some point during my manic struggle with fear, I realized I had a choice.

At some point during my manic struggle with fear, I realized I had a choice. I couldn't control everything, but I could control some things—such as the way I was fueling my imagination. I could allow my thoughts to run wild. I could let myself get so worked up that I could hear the wings crack and smell the burning engine. Or I could occupy my mind with other things, such as lyrics to my favorite classical hymns or words of Scripture reminding me He has my days already numbered.

But as I mentioned earlier, that annoying kid in the pool yelling "Watch me!" sometimes needs our attention. Troubling thoughts can move from uncomfortable to obsessive, and we need to know the difference.

Before my panic disorder was diagnosed and treated, the adrenaline in my system was out of control and made everything worse. Let's face it, adrenaline is a good thing when we're rescuing someone from drowning or if we're competing at Wimbledon, but it also makes relaxing very difficult. Being "anxious for nothing" becomes nearly impossible. Especially when social media and sensationalism make their living off our fears.

When my adrenaline problem was managed through heart medication, I could train my thoughts like a "normal" person. My doctor even suggested I get my pilot's license and educate myself on the safety of aerodynamics. Receiving practical advice for overcoming my fear was as much a part of renewing my mind as knowing my days are in God's hands. And this truth has transformed my thinking throughout the years.

I no longer live in fear of being hit by a meteor or struck by lightning. And though I realize both could happen, I no longer worry about it. God will either protect me from it or walk me through it. As the psalmist put it, "For he will command his angels concerning you to guard you in all your ways" (Psalm 91:11).

Or, should the plane crash, He will deliver me safely to His side and provide for those I've left behind and committed to Him. Either way, it's a win-win.

Fresh Eyes

My uncle loves telling the story about the time he sliced his hand open during one of his building projects. He was told he'd need stitches by a local doctor who was getting on in years. He cleaned my uncle's wound, stitched it up, and sent him on his way. On his return visit, the doctor made small talk while he removed my uncle's sutures. As he examined the wound, he commented that the gash had been deeper than he thought, but nothing like the guy who'd been in the week before. My uncle soon realized the old doctor was talking about him.

I'm not sure how much longer it was before the doc finally hung up his stethoscope, but I do know he left my uncle with a healthy scar and a great story to tell. It's a story that illustrates how perception and reality can be confused, though one hardly needs early dementia for that. Wounded emotions can easily do the trick.

Sometimes anger is appropriate, at least for a while. But bitterness that's left untreated can fester like an infected wound, destroying the healthy skin around it. Even the healthiest parts of our lives are not fully immune to resentment.

In Anne Lamott's book, coincidentally titled *Stitches: A Handbook on Meaning, Hope and Repair*, she talks about pain and our perception of it. Lamott has always written honestly about life's difficulties, including depression, alcoholism, and coming to terms with God. She targets one of our most serious threats to personal contentment—forgiving others. She points to C. S. Lewis, whose life, like Lamott's, was liberated when he discovered the relentless forgiveness of Christ. This forgiveness was left as an example for us to imitate, though we may need to start with baby steps. As C. S. Lewis put it in *Mere Christianity*, "If we really want to learn how to forgive, perhaps we had better start with something easier than the Gestapo."

In a world filled with frailties and failures, bitterness can feel like the best option.

In a world filled with frailties and failures, bitterness can feel like the best option. But if we want to move past the pain, forgiveness is the better reality. Sometimes it's the only thing that makes sense.

There are lots of things in life that don't make sense, such as whose cruel joke was it to put an S in the word lisp? Why is there braille on the buttons of drive-through ATMs? Why were we so eager for school to end when we were kids, just so we could go home and play school? Okay, maybe these aren't the kinds of mysteries that keep us awake at night, but the big stuff does, like the idea of forgiving someone who doesn't deserve it. It's one thing to forgive an infringement that was unintentional, but if it was deliberate, forget about it. All bets are off. It feels too good to hang on to our anger, even if it sucks the life right out of us.

Again, as with all things, forgiveness is all about perspective. It's about seeing things the way they are rather than how we *feel* they are. It's about asking what was behind the pain that was inflicted rather than letting the pain itself keep us up at night.

Empathy

Maybe one of the baby steps we can take during a conflict is tempering our perspective with a little empathy. Take politics, for example, a major source of discontentment in our culture. The political parties have become so polarized that remaining openminded or empathetic on any issue can seem impossible. Health care, the environment, immigration— they're all hot buttons.

As I went through the TSA line at the airport recently and was asked to step aside so they could check me over, I asked myself, *If the guys who flew the planes into the Twin Towers were Scandinavian, would I feel differently about this invasion of privacy? Would I be offended by the TSA taking a second look at my passport because I have blonde hair and blue eyes?* I don't think so, but then I've never been discriminated against.

Learning to see things from all angles isn't easy, especially when emotions are running high, but a little empathy can go a long way. Simply asking a person why he or she feels a certain way about something, and then actually listening to the answer, can relieve some of the pressure. Empathy is a key player in the game of getting along. And getting along is a key player in the game of contentment.

Chapter Five

PEOPLE
ARE WORK

In 1938, the Grant Study, the longest study of human development, began following the lives of Harvard University men. In the 1970s, it merged with a similar study that had begun in the 1940s but focused on less privileged young men from inner-city Boston tenements. Researchers periodically assessed the physical and emotional well-being of the study's participants. This helped them determine the impact of social status and upbringing on personal happiness. Robert Waldinger, a Harvard psychiatrist, took over the study in 2003 and shared his findings in a TED Talk he gave in 2015. So far, it's gotten thirteen million views.

Waldinger's takeaway was clear: those who maintain strong relationships, and not just romantic ones, are healthier and happier, regardless of their background or income.

Relationships tend to buffer us from the "slings and arrows" of growing old. On the other hand, brain function and overall health tends to deteriorate faster in those who isolate themselves, particularly by midlife. The results of the seventy-five-year-old study indicate that a good life is more than wealth, fame, and career success. Turns out money really can't buy happiness, though who among us wouldn't like to try?

Waldinger's findings include a caveat as well, one that speaks loudly to this generation. Casual relationships, such as those sustained only through social media, don't provide the same outcome.

Hmm . . .

As I read Waldinger's report, I realized that for some people, relationships are easier said than done. This is especially true for the "relationally challenged" among us, such as the introvert or the broken-hearted individual whose pain initiates solitude.

According to the research, the issue of "social anxiety" is much more far-reaching than first thought. The symptoms of Social Anxiety Disorder, or SAD (not to be confused with Seasonal Affective Disorder), include:

Fearing being around people or making conversation.
Being overly concerned about what others think
    of you.
Dreading a situation that involves other people
    for days.

Trembling, sweating, or feeling nauseated around
    other people.

Avoiding places where others will be.

Worrying about embarrassing yourself or offending
    others.

Having difficulty making and keeping friends.

Hmm . . .

Folks who care at all about what other people think
of them can probably find themselves somewhere on this
list. That's because caring is an
important social skill. The absence
of caring brings on a completely
different set of troubles.

Our connections with people are incredibly important, but they can also be a major source of discontentment.

Our connections with peo-
ple are incredibly important, but
they can also be a major source of
discontentment. This is especially
true with relationships we can't bow out of easily. It's one
thing if certain people annoy us and we can avoid them, or
somehow be "busy" every time they want to hang out. But
when those are not easy options, we're stuck. And feeling
trapped is hardly the stuff contentment is made of.

It's also hard to give up on a relationship we've invested
a lot into. Some difficult relationships are worth hanging
in there for, especially when we see people truly making an
effort. But let's face it, we tend to learn more from the bad

ones than we do from the good ones. Easy relationships are like cotton candy. They're pure sugar. Pure joy. And let me be clear, we do need our share of emotional sugar fixes. Because there will always be those who simply wear us out.

I love my kids equally but parenting them was very different. My son was the cotton candy, the sugar fix, the pleasure cruise. But my daughter taught me everything I know, specifically the survival skill of leaning into God. And, as I mentioned before, how *not* to be judgmental.

I have little tolerance for people who are prosperous and then determine the worth of others based on their position in life. They tend to complain about how unfair things are when bad things happen. But do they ever contemplate how unfair it is that good things have happened to them? Why should they have been given opportunities that others weren't?

I think we all benefit from taking seriously Luke 12:48, "Everyone to whom much was given, of him much will be required" (ESV). Especially when it comes to relationships.

The Other Grandma

We sort of expect adolescents to go through squirrelly phases as they grow up, but young people hardly have the corner on that market. My grandma taught me that. I loved spending time with my dad's mom, but she was a complicated woman. She was the grandma who "didn't go to church." The whole Christian thing wasn't sophisticated or intellectual enough for her. Ironically, she admired the likes of Dorothy Parker and others seated at the Algonquin Round Table whose stories didn't exactly end well.

Kudos to my mom for being decent enough to keep her wounds and resentments toward my grandma to herself, at least until I was an adult. There's usually no need to bad-mouth problem people, difficult family members, or ex-spouses. I've discovered that taking the high road usually allows these things to become clear to kids as they grow up, anyway, even without the trash talk. Still, as a child, my grandma captured my imagination. She smoked cigarettes from long slender holders. And bought me my first kiddie cocktail, a secret we kept from my Baptist mother. From her old photos, I imagined my grandma young, liberated, and looking very much like Norma Shearer from *The Women*. She said things I didn't hear anywhere else, things I wasn't sure I should repeat. But I liked spending time with her, and she liked me.

My mom's mom was another story. The experiences I had with her were completely different. The mere mention of her name still conjures up thoughts of chicken dinner after church, play clothes, and cousins. She was the grandma who prayed for us, the one whose house always smelled like warm bread and fresh coffee.

As I grew older, stories of my dad's mom began to filter down, and I started getting the picture. It was a portrait of hardship. Her mom had died when she was barely a teen, her father was abusive, and ultimately, she was shipped off to live with relatives. Then, just about the time life was coming together for her, tragedy struck again. She was on vacation with her husband, whom she adored, when he died suddenly of a brain aneurism. He was barely forty, and the pain through his head was a bolt of lightning he didn't survive.

My grandma never married again, and time didn't improve her. She became a difficult person to love, and her unkindness became legendary. One Christmas season my aunt Dot (my mom's sister) went to visit my grandma in her senior apartment building and happily announced that a group of carolers would be gathering to sing in the beautifully decorated lobby. But without missing a beat, and with complete sincerity, my dad's mom smiled and said, "Thank you, Dorothy. I'll be sure to close my door."

If we really want to reach the difficult people in our lives, we'll learn their dialect, we'll connect with them on their level, and we'll take our cues from their timing.

My dad's mom reminds me that most difficult people don't set out to be difficult. It's not a childhood dream to become addicted or abusive. But life happens, and like the rest of us, they have a choice to make. They can allow pain to consume them, dictate their actions, and tarnish their chances for contentment, or they can grab hold of it, reassess their situation, and adjust accordingly. Adjustment is the stuff contentment is made of.

Bad breaks are never made better by our bad choices. The truth is, my grandma was brought up by an aunt she loved very much. She gave birth to two beautiful, gifted twin boys, and she had grandkids to love. But she often resisted and allowed her pain to turn inward. Though she softened a bit in the end, basically, she died a very self-absorbed old woman.

Still, I'm glad my grandma and I connected as well as we did. She showed me a different angle to life and taught me how difficult people speak an entirely different language. Trying to communicate with them is frustrating. We get tired of walking on eggshells. We'd much rather wave our hands and say, "Forget it. You're an idiot. I'm done."

But if we really want to reach the difficult people in our lives, we'll learn their dialect, we'll connect with them on their level, and we'll take our cues from their timing. They don't need to fit into our box for us to love and accept them.

My grandma also taught me the secret of how *not* to be wounded by a difficult person. I expected nothing from her, so she never disappointed me. Instead, I was fed emotionally and spiritually by my other grandma, which freed me to enjoy my dad's mom simply for who she was—as imperfect as the rest of us, but definitely worth loving.

The Problem with People

Here's the thing: even the best relationships take effort. That's why understanding what makes other people difficult can be just as important as understanding what makes us difficult. Our expectations of people need to be tempered by healthy doses of reality.

I was weeks away from graduating with a degree in elementary education when I made a disturbing discovery about myself. I realized I don't even like kids. Well, not enough to teach them anyway. Sensing this might be a problem, I never taught them. Instead, I discovered a passion for teaching adults. It's kind of funny when I think back to the evaluation I was given for my student teaching. It said something like, "Ann has what it takes to be a good teacher, and the kids really like her, but something's missing." *You think?*

In retrospect, I didn't babysit kids very often. I wasn't particularly fond of caring for newborns, either. Thankfully, both of mine survived, but I like babies when they get all chubby and durable, like around nine months.

My sister, on the other hand, was always a natural with newborns. She'd grab her babies and head out for the afternoon equipped only with a diaper and a pacifier. Easy breezy. For me, though, going out was a major production. An afternoon outing meant a diaper bag stuffed with bottles, blankets, and bulb syringes . . . just in case.

I remember the day my sister told me she wanted to do some foster care for newborns. With her three kids now in school, she thought she'd enjoy caring for babies from their delivery to the time of their adoption. I couldn't think of anything worse, which is sort of how my sister feels when she thinks about me speaking in front of a thousand people. Different people, different gifts.

The day Lisa arrived, my sister's house exploded with joy. It was love at first sight. Lisa's soft brown face framed with jet black curls already set her apart from the rest of the towheaded crew, but she also had Down syndrome, a fact my sister's family tended to forget. However, days turned into weeks and weeks into months, and no calls came inquiring about adopting Lisa. But, clearly, something else was happening too.

We don't need people's approval either, which is tricky for those of us born with a "tell me I'm good" sign pinned to our back.

One morning the phone call I'd been expecting finally came. My sister's family wanted to adopt Lisa. It seemed they'd all fallen in love with one another and couldn't imagine life without her.

I'll admit I had my reservations. What would caring for Lisa look like when she was no longer wrapped neatly in a newborn blanket? I couldn't imagine. But then I realized why. God hadn't given me the vision for this mission. He had given it to my sister's family, along with the assurance He would provide. Then, toward the end of our conversation, my sister said the words that sealed Lisa's fate. They were words that could have come from the lips of Jesus Himself. "If we don't love her, who will?"

Lisa's life is a testimony to broken dreams put back

together. She is a constant reminder of who we are. She may never become all the things a mom might hope for her daughter, but my sister sees beyond all that—the same way God looks at us. The fact is, not everyone is cut out for business management, foreign missions, or even motherhood. And recognizing that fact, in ourselves and in others, can be very liberating.

I remember listening to an old woman pray when I was very young. She said, "Lord, please give me an eternal perspective." I've grown to appreciate this kind of prayer. God sees beyond our limitations and shortcomings and loves us anyway. We are His adopted children, He says, not the ones He's "stuck with" but the ones He chooses.

Getting Along

People can be challenging even under the best of circumstances. And here's another newsflash: we don't need to agree with everything a person thinks before we can get along with him or her. We don't need people's approval either, which is tricky for those of us born with a "tell me I'm good" sign pinned to our back. As we look at the world today, it may feel as though people are disagreeing more than ever. But as one who has studied history, I can assure you people have always battled each other. It's just that now we have Twitter feeds and social media keeping turmoil constantly in our face.

Disagreements have been around since people could form opinions. It was just easier in prehistoric times to hunker down in your cozy cave and cut yourself off from the other Neanderthals who drove you crazy. These days, it's hard to escape the twenty-four-hour news feeds that keep us polarized and constantly on edge. And with political correctness running amok, disagreeing with anyone about anything is grounds for being labeled narrow-minded. The term "closed-minded" has been completely redefined since I was in college. It's no longer enough to respect people and their freedom of choice. We have to agree with them, otherwise we are a bigot, a racist, or a transphobic.

My sister-in-law's marriage to her partner coincided with the Supreme Court's landmark decision to legalize same-sex marriage. As they tied the knot, I thought about how the media had talked about little else for months. But as discussions continued, both in the news and around the watercooler, I began to wonder if I'd missed something. When did holding a different opinion about anything automatically make someone wrong? When did simply seeing something differently make you a bigot?

Obviously, disagreeing with someone can become extreme, hate-filled, and even violent. But so can the other extreme—the one that says we should all agree. Think *Mein Kampf*. Most sensible people can hold a different opinion without attacking anyone or wishing them harm. This is the stuff democracy is built on, as Evelyn Beatrice Hall pointed out. The English biographer of Voltaire famously wrote, "I disapprove of what you say, but I will defend to the death your right to say it."

Freedom of thought and freedom of speech are good things, but let's face it, they can be complicated. News programs that inform us can inflame us too. But the clamor of disagreement shouldn't trouble us too much. In fact, it should be music to our ears—the wheels of democracy in motion keeping any one school of thought from squelching the freedom of another.

> The question should be how to disagree with someone and still show love.

I remember when Mike Ditka, the former head coach of the Chicago Bears, was forced to make his restaurant and sports bar in downtown Chicago smoke-free. As I listened to him defend his right to run his establishment the way he wanted to, I found myself agreeing with him. And, just for the record, I can speak with complete objectivity. First, I don't smoke. Second, I don't drink. And third, and probably most significantly, I am not a Chicago Bears fan. I cheer for Green Bay.

So, I was able to listen to the coach's arguments with a completely open mind. And thirty minutes into his speech at the three-hour city council meeting, I found myself strangely drawn to his side of every argument. He spoke on behalf of the hospitality, restaurant, and liquor industries and said, "Don't impose the will of the few on the lives of the many."

Hear, hear. No one is forcing anyone to visit Ditka's restaurant. But if they want to risk their health and beautiful white teeth to chew on a cigar, that should be up to them. As Americans, we embrace the freedoms we enjoy, but when topics turn to health care, global warming, or gay marriage, we're not sure how to respond. And arguing becomes even more contentious when we're not clear about the terms we use to debate.

Millennials, for the most part, have backed candidates with a socialist agenda in recent decades. To them, the word socialism means equality and taking care of the less fortunate. But for those of us who have been studying history a little bit longer, socialism conjures up memories of human rights abuses and names such as Karl Marx, Friedrich Engels, and Vladimir Lenin.

So, pick your poison. Everyone disagrees about something, unless they're comatose. Clearly, we've all known people who have chosen to be unkind and closed-minded when they disagree. But, as I've pointed out many times, no one has a corner on the idiot market either. There's plenty of stupidity to go around. The question should be how to disagree with someone and still show love. Or, more specifically, for those of us who crave validation, how to live comfortably knowing someone disagrees with us.

It's hard to feel content when our opinions get vetoed,

particularly when we believe it's our job to save the world. There are lots of reasons people may disagree with us, the least of which is because they don't like us (unless we are real jerks). It all boils down to respect. And as a believer, I think God places a high premium on how much we respect each other. "Do nothing out of selfish ambition or vain conceit. Rather, in humility value others above yourselves" (Philippians 2:3).

Chapter Six

CHECK YOUR JUDGMENT AT THE DOOR

Our struggle with self-image is another huge source of discontentment. It's also a bit of a balancing act. When we focus too much on it, we become self-absorbed, and no one can stand us. When we overlook it altogether, we feel like a loser and suck the wind out of everyone's sails.

To begin with, it's hard to see ourselves the way we *actually* are. We're much more comfortable with our virtual selves. Just look at what we post on Facebook and Instagram. And it's hard to be objective, even when we really try. I mean, who doesn't prefer the elongated mirrors at the mall that make every pair of jeans we squeeze into look fabulous?

The whole concept of self-image is a mystery too. I've often wondered why some people seem to have an enormous amount of self-confidence when it seems they shouldn't, and vice versa. I read an article about Demi Moore, who admitted to struggling with a negative self-image. With her long dark hair, those big brown eyes, and a body chiseled to perfection, who'd ever suspect that she, along with a lot of other Hollywood stars, battles insecurity?

Then there are those who overestimate their assets, as my girlfriend discovered when she wandered onto a nude beach in Europe . . . purely by accident, mind you. She quickly realized those beaches are populated by all the wrong people.

Our struggle with self-image is another huge source of discontentment.

Everyone struggles with body image. Well, maybe not the nude-beach gang. But for the rest of us, women especially, it's an issue. I've never put much stock in dream therapy, but some of my dreams certainly reflect my insecurities. I'll often dream I'm sitting in a large auditorium at a conference, sipping coffee and relaxing. Then, suddenly, I'm informed that I'm the keynote speaker. Naturally, I have nothing prepared, I have no notes, and, for some reason, I can't remember any of my talks . . . not a word. My fear is I'll look ridiculous.

The hormone-fueled dreams I had while I was pregnant with my first child wouldn't have taken Freud long to analyze. Obviously, my fears were close to the surface because I kept dreaming I misplaced my newborn. He was the size of a peanut, and I kept looking for him in the couch cushions and under the rug. I couldn't keep track of him, and I realized I was a terrible mom.

Another pregnancy dream I had was just as obvious. I dreamt I was sitting in the waiting room at the hospital while my mom went through labor for me. When it was finally time to push, the nurse came out to get me. I put the magazine down, headed to the birthing room, and switched places with my mom.

Even when I'm not pregnant I tend to have crazy dreams. One reoccurring dream exposes more than my insecurities. I'm usually out in public, walking down the street or strolling through a mall, and I'm extremely uncomfortable, but I don't know why. Then, I suddenly realize I'm topless. Obviously, I left home in such a hurry that I neglected to finish dressing.

I was having dinner with a group of friends, and we started discussing some of our crazy dreams. I shared my reoccurring dream about being horrified to discover I'm topless out in public. Then I added the strange little twist my dream always includes. Although I'm totally mortified to discover I'm topless, no one else around me seems to notice. Ironically, one of the guys at the table was a plastic surgeon. He laughed with the rest of us, then said, "Well, Ann, that's where I come in. I'll make them notice."

I laughed, too, but later I got to thinking. I was only in my thirties at the time, but I wondered if I would ever feel society's pressure to remain young or be beautiful at any cost. I'm all for people doing what they can to feel good about themselves. I work out, highlight my hair, and use whitening toothpaste. And I'm rarely seen without something on my lips. But I've also seen women who, in their last-ditch effort to hold on to youthful beauty, have allowed their faces to be completely contorted. It's unsettling, but I do understand their panic.

Men have their hang-ups, too, but typically they don't struggle with body image the same way women do. I mean, really, how many men do you know who stand in front of a mirror for thirty minutes or ask their friends if their jeans make their butts look big?

I'm not sure why there's such a difference between men and women, but Rachel Simmons, the cofounder of the Girls Leadership Institute, offers some insight. She believes men are better conditioned to face the fact that there will always be someone who's better, faster, and stronger. Girls, on the other hand, are subtly conditioned to take very few risks. So, they tend to engage in activities where they know they'll succeed. Simmons believes this explains why, statistically, we have so few women in male-dominated careers, such as the tech jobs in Silicon Valley.

Girls can be brutal on themselves and others. They point out every imperfection they can find, especially the physical ones. But again, unless we're competing for Miss Universe or a place on the runway, *most* people don't see their own imperfections the way others do, particularly men.

I heard two guys beautifully illustrate this point on a radio interview. One guy told the story of how he'd recently stepped out of the shower, and as he toweled down, he noticed his wife lying on the bed watching TV. In order to get dressed, he realized he'd have to pass in front of her to get his clothes from the closet.

He had a choice to make.

He could stay wrapped up in his towel, walk to the closet, get dressed, and then go back to the bathroom to hang up his towel. Or he could save himself a trip by hanging up his towel first, then walking to the closet, thus passing in front of his wife in all his glory.

Politically correct or not, things are just different with men and women.

Slightly overconfident, he chose the latter. But the moment he stepped into the bedroom, he knew he'd chosen poorly when his wife said, "Honey, please. Cover up."

I suppose there are lots of women who wouldn't mind the free show, but this story beautifully illustrates how men and women see things differently. This was confirmed even further when the guy explained why he'd chosen the way he did. He said the real reason he walked in front of his wife naked was because he knew how much he'd enjoy it if she'd do the same. He was just returning the favor, so to speak. Paying it forward.

Clearly, there's beauty in the male frame. Think of

Michelangelo's *David*. But, honestly, what's with these men we hear about in the news who send texts of their private parts to women? *Really?* Next time send a box of chocolates.

Politically correct or not, things are just different with men and women. I was speaking to a group of young moms recently and reminded them of these differences. I encouraged them to make it work for them and told them to ease up on themselves. The fact that men see things differently is good news, especially for those women discontented with their bodies, who dive under the covers and insist on killing the lights. I encouraged them to relax a bit and sing along with the new bride in the Song of Songs. "I belong to my beloved, and his desire is for me" (7:10). Because remember, two things happen when a woman undresses in front of a man: she becomes self-conscious, and he becomes grateful.

Competition

Comparing ourselves to others can be another serious blow to our sense of contentment. If we're not directly competing with friends, coworkers, or the other soccer parents, we're competing with the beautiful people we see splashed all over social media with perfect bodies, perfect families, and hundreds of likes.

Okay. I'll admit it. When I was a young mom, I went through a phase where I read every Danielle Steel book I could get my hands on. It was pure escapism. But, eventually, I began to realize that my mind was being shaped by the subtleties of the author's pen.

Steel's glossy pages made my life seem boring in comparison. My husband and kids didn't stand a chance. It was sort of the same thing when I read Frank Peretti's novel *This Present Darkness*. His words were so vivid, they stirred up a kind of paranoia that caused me to "see" demonic forces at work *evvvverywhere*.

> Comparing ourselves to others can be another serious blow to our sense of contentment.

And the competition among us is worse than ever.

In the olden days people just lived. They spent their energy building, farming, and surviving. In fact, I've often wondered what my grandparents would think if they saw the rows of treadmills at the gym filled with people running absolutely nowhere. All that wasted energy. I was just waiting for someone to invent a treadmill that converts our energy into something really useful, like an air conditioner or a fully charged iPod.

According to old photos, women in my grandma's day wore housecoats by the age of thirty-five. Who cared what was under there? But now our Western culture has become a breeding ground for personal discontent.

Just think: millions of dollars are spent every day convincing us our teeth are not white enough, our clothes are not bright enough, our detergent is not strong enough, and our deodorant doesn't last long enough. It's kind of creepy, but there are people who actually go to work thinking of ways to make us feel bad about ourselves, just so we'll buy their products.

In college, my daughter wrote a paper titled "Self-Image and the Media." Her research included thumbing through dozens of magazines with pictures of girls who, without makeup and coifing, would appear to have just escaped from Auschwitz.

Evidently, a few extra pounds have become the new scourge in our day . . . the leprosy of our time. But who can compete with a fashion model whose shoulders and legs are routinely photoshopped? How can we live with any real sense of contentment in a culture that uses horrific terms like "heroin chic"?

Insecurities

Several years ago, after I spoke at a conference, a mom pulled me aside to talk about her sons who were both in middle school. The older one was popular. No problem there. But the younger one struggled. He was awkward, often teased, and from a very early age had a knack for saying all the wrong things at all the wrong times. Tears filled her eyes as she told me that while riding in the car recently, through his sobs he asked, "Why did God make me like this?" I felt her pain as I thought about how our childhood insecurities feed our adult discontent.

Recently, I drove by my own grade school . . . the breeding ground of my personal insecurities, and for some reason, fourth-grade reading class came to mind. I wasn't a fast reader and dreaded the timed assessment tests that grouped me with the other slow readers in class. The teachers tried to be diplomatic, using innocuous group names, like Cardinals, Blue Jays, or Robins. But it took us less than three seconds to decode that.

The memory was a minor annoyance compared to the wounds I'm regularly told about—the wounds that cut much deeper. I didn't grow up with the fear of ridicule and rejection. Still, I was reminded of how fragile we all are as I drove to the back of the school and looked at the playground that seemed much bigger in retrospect.

My mind jumped to fifth grade and the little girl who seemed to run the place. She was a powerful little thing and made life miserable for me. I tried to win her over so that by default her friends would become my friends too—a game some of us never outgrow. And, initially, it worked. I invited her to the movies and brought her with me to youth group. My mom even threw in a trip to the ice cream place for good measure. But my plan worked so well, it actually backfired. Little Miss Playground quickly sensed a threat to her position as her friends began to like me too. She had to work fast.

One night she crafted a carefully worded document that

had my name written across the top. It said something like, "We hate Ann. She's fat and ugly and stupid, and nobody here likes her." Then she went around the entire fifth grade and got as many kids to sign it as she could.

The next morning, she met me at the playground and handed me the paper. As I read the document, I felt a knife slowly twist in my heart. I knew the words were legally binding. I believed every one. Refusing to let her see me cry, I fought back the tears, then escaped to the bathroom.

As I drove away from the old playground, I realized this happened more than three decades ago. Yet, I could conjure up the pain as though it were yesterday. Ironically, that little girl went on to become one of my oldest friends, still feeling guilty over her unkindness to me. But I tell her I probably have her to thank for turning me into a lifelong runner. But what strikes me most about my story is this: if some silly playground drama can cut so deeply, how much more deeply can the words of a parent, a spouse, or a trusted friend cut? It's not easy to erase words such as *fat*, *ugly*, and *stupid*. *Loser*, *idiot*, *mistake*.

And this was before social media. In the olden days, when our feelings were crushed, we nursed our wounds privately and moved on. Now, cyberspace has become a launching pad for bullying with words and images that can be hard to delete. My mom used to say, "Be careful with your words, because once they've been spoken, they can never fully be taken back." Even when we're sorry.

For most of us, our self-image will tend to evolve. By the time I entered high school, I never saw myself as a ravishing beauty, but I did all right. However, looking back, I don't think I understood what real beauty looks like. I had my share of hang-ups as a teenager and never quite made peace with my chubby cheeks. (In retrospect, it's a miracle my daughter didn't develop an eating disorder because of my hang-ups. Obviously, if it had been left up to me, she would have.)

When my husband and I were dating, I was happy to learn he'd been painfully thin as a kid. I figured if I married him, maybe my kids' cheeks would stand a chance. I'd buy their jeans from the slim-cut department and threaten them if they didn't finish every bite on their plate.

One night he even told me he tried everything to gain weight, including the consumption of five Big Macs in one sitting. Then he chased it down with a large chocolate shake.

That sounded like a marriage proposal to me.

But when my kids entered the world, they were more gorgeous than I could have imagined, even with my cheeks. They were strong and sturdy. They came from beautiful Scandinavian stock, bred to weather the harshest of winters while everyone around them dropped dead.

When I was a freshman in high school, I dated an upperclassman who was a football player and cute enough for my friends to be jealous. But it wasn't until second semester that my concept of "beauty" was changed forever. On the first day of the second semester, we were given our new schedules and set out to find our classes. My fourth-hour study hall was back in the shop area where tables of four were set up and waiting. When I got there, my three table-mates were already seated. Two of them I hardly knew. The third was a boy I'd never seen before, another upperclass-man. In my depth of character, I immediately sized him up and determined nothing about him attracted me. So, I took my seat convinced the entire study hall would be a bust . . . because who actually studied back then?

However, to my surprise, as the weeks rolled by and I was forced to sit next to this long, lanky stranger, he began to grow on me. His soft-spoken style and clever wit caught me completely off guard. He was clearly one of the brightest boys I'd ever talked to, and fourth hour was quickly becom-ing the highlight of my day.

Fast-forward to the conference where I listened to the troubled mom tell me about her struggling son. Negative messages get thrown at us from every direction. And when we're young, the seeds of insecurity take root deep inside our psyche, producing all sorts of tender shoots. Feeling the weight of her pain, I listened and chose my words carefully. Yes, developing a good sense of ourselves is an ongoing bat-tle. By then I'd met a lot of people who wouldn't be classi-fied as "attractive" by society's standards. But I'd noticed something about them—the ones who hadn't been able to coast along on their good looks or sex appeal: they were the ones who engaged me most, probably because they'd had to hone in on their other assets, such as kindness, intelligence, creativity, and humor. Those were the people I wanted to spend my time with.

There's always someone who wants to criticize how we act, how we dress, or how we worship.

This is good news because it means beauty is within everyone's grasp.

Contentment is never about being the best *someone else* can be. It's about being the best *we* can be within our own unique strengths and weaknesses. Genuine beauty doesn't come from the smoke and mirrors of L'Oréal and Revlon (though they can help soften some of the rough edges). Beauty is about finding the sweet spot in our own beautiful mess and making it shine.

I encouraged the mom to help her son mine the nuggets of beauty he was most certainly created with. She should help him discover for himself his own beautiful purpose, confident that he too is "fearfully and wonderfully made" (Psalm 139:14).

Push Back

It takes effort to push back against the strong opinions of others. There's always someone who wants to criticize how we act, how we dress, or how we worship. This is made even tougher in the age of political correctness. PC has more than replaced the Golden Rule; it has started to dictate how we should think. And if we don't conform, we're seen as narrow-minded and bigoted . . . which is strangely ironic. How does conforming make someone open-minded?

Let's face it, sometimes we just need to be free to think for ourselves. Svend Brinkmann, a Danish professor of psychology in the Department of Communication and Psychology at Aalborg University, thinks so. He's tired of being told we need to improve, conform, think positive, and listen to our inner voice.

I first heard him interviewed when he released his book, *Stand Firm: Resisting the Self-Improvement Craze*. It's sort of a self-help book on how to ignore self-help books. According to Brinkmann, we need to resist today's obsession with introspection and self-improvement.

Navel gazing? Sometimes there's nothing in there.

Perpetual positivity? Sometimes being grumpy makes sense.

Saying yes to everyone? Sometimes no is the right answer.

The description for Brinkmann's book explains that "the secret to a happier life lies not in finding your inner self but in that coming to terms with yourself is how to coexist peacefully with others. Not finding ourselves."

Hear, hear.

Mark Manson, an American self-help author, blogger, and entrepreneur, takes a slightly different approach in his book, *The Subtle Art of Not Giving a [. . .]: A Counterintuitive Approach to Living a Good Life.* Like Brinkmann, Manson, a purveyor of profanity and blunt honesty, reacts to the "self-help" industry with, again ironically, a self-help book of his own. Manson finds the "mindless positivity" touted in many self-improvement guides to be impractical and unhelpful to most people.

Personally, I think both authors are onto something. I don't agree with everything they say, but in this hyper-PC world, I'm feeling the heat like everyone else. I consider myself to be as conscientious as anyone else. I think everyone's opinion is valuable, and I also try to follow the rules. But therein lies the problem. The rules keep changing. I can't scroll through Facebook without feeling guilty about something . . . the food I eat, the car I drive, my choice of toilet paper.

I particularly liked Brinkmann's sixth step to resisting the self-improvement craze of our time. (His book offers seven.) He instructs us to put down the self-help book and pick up a novel instead. Great advice. "[Self-help books] always top the bestseller lists, but often they just . . . reinforce the idea that life is something we control. . . . Ultimately, they leave you despondent at your failure to realize their myriad promises of happiness, wealth and health. Novels, on the other hand, enable you to understand human life as complex and unmanageable."[1]

One of the benefits of getting older, and there are a few,

is gaining the kind of confidence and balance that comes from having made a few trips around the block. I don't exactly want to turn into one of those old geezers who really doesn't give a rip what people think. On the other hand, living to please others is exhausting.

Eureka Moments

I love "Eureka!" moments. The big "Duh, how could I have missed that?" moments. Not that every revelation is comfortable. Sometimes self-discovery is extremely uncomfortable. But how else can change begin?

The *New York Times* recently reported about the eureka-moment findings of Judith Moskowitz, a professor of medical social sciences at Northwestern University. Her research uncovered eight skills that build positive emotions, improve our quality of life, and maybe even add years to our lives.

At the University of California, Moskowitz studied people in crisis and observed their ability to feel calm and happy, even during dire circumstances. She and her colleagues found that people with AIDS, type 2 diabetes, and other chronic illnesses lived longer when they remained positive. They tended to stay connected with friends, followed their doctor's orders, and embraced a healthier lifestyle with these eight skills, including noticing a daily positive event and keeping a gratitude journal.[2]

Moskowitz was encouraged by her findings, and I was too. I've been teaching these principles for years, and now there's empirical evidence to give them cachet. Studies indicate that when patients try to practice these eight skills, their immune levels are stronger, and they're less likely to suffer depression. And you can't argue with science, right?

Sometimes we get so entrenched in our discontentment that it's hard to see something good, even when it's right in front of us. Eureka moments are those pleasant surprises that remind us of the evidence that has been there all along.

Moskowitz's findings remind me of a very cool eureka moment found in the New Testament. It's a story recorded by Luke, a physician and part-time journalist, and it speaks to the mystery of discovery. Why is it hard to see things as they really are?

Jesus was walking along the road to Emmaus and came upon two of his followers who were visibly shaken by the crucifixion. To them, a dream had died. Jesus knew what was on their minds, but he asked them to tell him what they were upset about. Not recognizing Jesus, one of them answered, "Are you the only visitor to Jerusalem who does not know the things that have happened there in these days?" (Luke 24:18).

They began telling Jesus about the prophet from Nazareth who was "powerful in word and deed" before God and all the people (v. 19). He was sentenced to death, crucified, and buried. And now, to make matters worse, his body was missing from the tomb.

Jesus responded by offering the kind of comfort a perfect eureka moment provides. He used their own Scriptures, centuries old, to highlight truth that had been there all along. He said, "How foolish you are, and how slow to believe all that the prophets have spoken! Did not the Messiah have to suffer these things and enter his glory?" (v. 25).[3]

Then, using their Scriptures, Jesus began with Moses and moved through the prophets, showing them what had been foretold about His coming centuries before. And their eyes were opened, which is exactly the part of Luke's story I wonder about (v. 31).

What makes us unable to recognize something that's right in front of us? Grief? Fear? Prejudice? Writing a book on the topic of doubt introduced me to the mind of the skeptic. Sometimes, as I'd listen to the angry words of an atheist, I'd think, Wow. Their unbelief sounds stronger than my belief. There was never any room for wonder and discovery, which is exactly what damaged emotions can do to us. Mind closed. End of story.

Pain traps us and keeps us from discovering all sorts of opportunities, people, and places. Keeping our eyes open when they'd prefer to remain shut takes effort. It's like coming out of a matinee after being isolated by the darkness of a movie theater for two hours. Our eyes want to stay closed, but we force them open so we won't walk into traffic.

Can We Change?

The problem is, we can feel stuck in a behavior or a thought pattern and begin to wonder if change is even possible. But are we doomed to a prewritten script?

This is the kind of question scientists and philosophers love to kick around. Though if The Verve's lyrics are any indication, there's probably very little hope of us changing—with even less hope of us getting their hit song, "Bitter Sweet Symphony," out of our head.

> I can't change, I can't change, I can't change…
> I can't change my mold, no, no, no, no, no, no, no.

Actually, the answer to whether a person can change is pretty significant and has some serious ramifications. I mean, if we can't change, how can we be held responsible for our behavior? Can a negative pattern be broken?

In 2001, Andrea Yates confessed to methodically drowning her five children in the bathtub. Then she carried them to the bedroom and laid them on the bed. Her defense was insanity. Obviously, right? Not so fast. If Gibbs has taught us anything on *NCIS*, it's that securing an "innocent by reason of insanity" verdict is next to impossible. The defendant must prove he or she couldn't discern right from wrong at the time of the crime.

Was Yates crazy or simply evil? She had been under a doctor's care for "very severe" postpartum depression, but her actions showed forethought. She had an hour before her mother-in-law would arrive, and she locked up the family dog before committing her gruesome crime.

Yates was found guilty in Texas, a state where capital punishment is legal, but she was given life instead. I remember hearing the verdict and thinking, *Wow. If she isn't insane, who among us is?* Eventually, in 2006, she was found "not guilty by reason of insanity" and committed to a mental hospital. So, what changed?

Robert Sapolsky is a neuroendocrinologist and professor of biology at Stanford University. He believes people are highly evolved and simply react to their genetics and upbringing. There are "neurological reasons" why people engage in high-risk behavior. When asked in an interview if people can change, I thought Sapolsky might break into The Verve's "Bitter Sweet Symphony." But his response was simply, "No. Not really."

At the other end of the spectrum is Nadine Burke Harris, also a researcher and a woman of science. As a pediatrician, Harris has extensively studied the connection between trauma in a person's life and their biology. While working in a "low-income, underserved" area of San Francisco, Harris began seeing an uptick in health issues in kids who came from families where violence and drug addiction were prevalent.

Harris tells about a mom who brought her child in for asthma. When Harris asked the mom if she saw a pattern in the child's flare-ups, the mom thought about it for a minute, then said, "It does seem to get worse when my husband hits the wall with his fist."

Harris's findings are among a growing body of evidence that suggests that the effects of childhood trauma can change a person's very DNA. This is where science comes in. Harris says trauma can impact various control centers of the brain, including the centers for pleasure and reward and impulse control. Repeated trauma can keep the stress response system in hyperdrive, flooding the body with hormones that, over time, inhibit the body's ability to read and transcribe its DNA. What Harris is saying, in layman's terms, is that external influences *can* rewrite the brain's script. Early detection and screening are our best lines of defense. Equipping ourselves to counter risk factors is important too. And we can all be taught how to reduce our stressors through intervention, therapy, and/or medication.[4]

Recognizing that life is a process that ebbs and flows frees us up to stay in the game without giving up.

The ability to develop new patterns is something I see evidence of every day—in my own life and in the lives of those I work with. The obstacles may seem greater these days, but the resources available are also better than ever. Anxiety is nothing new, but the intensity of our contemporary world does present us with an entirely new set of challenges . . . which is the bad news. But the good news is that our high-tech culture also brings with it an excellent set of tools that can help us deal more effectively with the pressures of modern living.

This is where a good "toolbox" comes in handy. We don't need to stay trapped in the past, but we can make use of it to inform our future. This is what redemption is all about. God's grace can reach into our lives and change our entire trajectory. Having overcome a panic disorder to become a public speaker makes me living proof of that.

Life isn't tidy, and the obsession to make it so will only frustrate us further. I think that's what Jesus meant in Matthew 11 when he addressed a crowd bogged down by life. The religious leaders of the day kept adding rules to the playbook and making life more complicated. So, in response, Jesus said, "Come to me, all you who are weary and burdened, and I will give you rest. Take my yoke upon you and learn from me. . . . For my yoke is easy, and my burden is light" (vv. 28-30).

Yes, please.

Recognizing that life is a process that ebbs and flows frees us up to stay in the game without giving up. It gives us permission to appreciate the differences in others while charting our *own* course and enjoying our *own* journey.

It also allows us the flexibility we need to mess up and start over again, which can be a daily ritual for some. I'm glad Lamentations 3:22-23 tells us that God's mercies are new *every* morning. Great is His faithfulness.

Chapter Seven

TRENDSETTERS

I. Spirit (our spiritual act of worship)

Holistic Superhero Trending

These days, everything is about being *holistic*. Nutrition. Education. Health care. But thousands of years before it was trending, the apostle Paul laid out a very holistic approach to contentment. Obviously he was a bit of a trendsetter. Who knew?

In his letter to the church in Rome, Paul points out the spirit-body-mind connection and emphasizes the importance of each one. Sounding very much like the spiritual leader he was, Paul says, "Therefore, I urge you, brothers and sisters, in view of God's mercy, to offer your bodies as a living sacrifice, holy and pleasing to God—this is your [spiritual act of] worship. Do not conform to the pattern of this world, but be transformed by the renewing of your mind. Then you will be able to test and approve what God's will is—his good, pleasing and perfect will" (Romans 12:1-2).

> Our spiritual *act of worship is to offer our* bodies *and renew our* minds.

Notice the threefold connection: our *spiritual* act of worship is to offer our *bodies* and renew our *minds*. Paul reminds us that we are multidimensional beings, so the solutions to our problems need to be multidimensional as well. This includes our struggle with discontentment. Paul begins by pointing out the importance of our spiritual life. It's as though he realizes we need to be reminded we have one. Most of us don't think about our daily lives in spiritual terms. We cook dinner. We chase kids. We write sales reports. It all feels pretty basic and earthy. So, recognizing our tendency to overlook the spiritual side of things, the apostle Paul reminds us in Colossians 3:23 that everything we do is "as unto the Lord" (ASV). Everything. This puts an obvious spin on things, like sitting in rush-hour traffic or doing a third load of laundry.

Thinking beyond the immediate demands of life takes

effort, which is why meditation has become so trendy. In our crazy-busy manic culture, slowing down simply to breathe sounds revolutionary. But these days, all this trendiness may cost you. One million dollars, to be exact, if you want some one-on-one training time with America's top motivational guru, Tony Robbins. You'll have to wait your turn too. While speaking at a three-day event in Florida, the best-selling author, whose high-profile clients include Serena Williams and Hugh Jackman, told the crowd there is a five-year waiting list.

To his credit, though, the guy with the big smile recognized that most of us will find his fees a little steep. So, via Facebook stream, he generously offered a free strategy to equip us to meet life's demands effectively. He calls it "priming."

Thinking beyond the immediate demands of life takes effort.

"If you're going to get the results that you deserve and that you want, you want to prime yourself for success," Robbins says. "You need a daily practice—a daily practice that's going to put you in the best state possible, regularly. Prime yourself for courage. The most important muscles that change your life are those mental, emotional, spiritual muscles."[1]

According to Robbins, ten minutes in the morning is all we need to follow these two steps:

> 1. Make time for reflection, gratitude, and mindful breathing.
> 2. Read or listen to a book that inspires and helps you overcome.

Robbins believes these two simple steps will "clarify us" and equip us to face the challenges of our day. But as I read the advice, two things jumped out at me: "There is nothing new under the sun," as Solomon pointed out three thousand years ago (Ecclesiastes 1:9). Also, I don't charge nearly enough.

Tony Robbins may be all the rage right now, but thirty-five years ago, it was Robert McKain, an estate planner from Connecticut. He wrote the best-selling book *How to Get to the Top and Stay There*. This inspired Stephen Covey to write his classic book *The 7 Habits of Highly Effective People*, and on it goes.

One of the benefits of getting older is processing enough life to gain some perspective.

Again, one of the benefits of getting older is processing enough life to gain some perspective. There may be nothing new under the sun, but a good principle is a good principle, and a timeless truth is worth repeating, especially when it's given a makeover. Things just sound more profound when we use words such as *mindfulness* and *transcendental meditation* (TM for short).

Stretching our bodies sounds much more interesting when it's called yoga.

Trendy or not, my grandma was way ahead of her time, and she didn't even know what TM meant. With a moment to herself, and a Bible on her lap, she just called it "quiet time." And it didn't cost her a thing.

All Things Eastern

Familiarity has a way of breeding contempt. We get bored with our jobs, our kids, our houses, and our spouses. We know that if the grass looks greener on the other side of the fence we should water our own lawn, but sometimes the spigot runs dry. Even our religion can begin to feel a bit stale.

When I was young, I remember thinking how boring my church was compared to the others in the neighborhood. They had steeple bells and stained-glass windows. I wanted candles and incense. I wanted mysterious looking nuns who wore black dresses and beads. I wanted to cross myself when I prayed.

For those of us living in America who grew up going to Sunday school, the West can't hold a candle to the East. People like Deepak Chopra have been able to cash in on our fascination with all things Eastern. He broke into our cultural consciousness looking very exotic, especially to those of us reared on Wonder Bread. His involvement with

Transcendental Meditation led him to an encounter with Maharishi Mahesh Yogi in the 1980s. He moved to California where he was an endocrinologist by profession and a Hindu by faith. But Chopra broke from the TM movement in 1994, claiming the Maharishi's approach had become too "cultish." He wanted to be taken seriously.

The Maharishi, on the other hand, claimed that Chopra's approaches not only rivaled his own, but demanded far too much money. In fact, according to *The San Diego Union-Tribune*, Chopra's net worth is about $80 million.[2]

Truth may not be trendy, but it is a game changer.

Compare Chopra's story with that of Ravi Zacharias, a philosopher and apologist by profession and a Christian by faith. He too was born in India and brought up as a Hindu around the same time as Chopra. Zacharias began his work in Vietnam in the early 1970s working with American soldiers, POWs, and the Viet Cong. This work launched an extensive international career that, today, as one journalist puts it, follows in the footsteps of Christian intellectuals such as C. S. Lewis and G. K. Chesterton. "Zacharias has positioned himself in the rocky seas of religious academia, and that is exactly where he wants to be: a classical evangelist in the arena of the intellectually resistant."[3]

Though it hasn't afforded him the same kind of fame and fortune Chopra enjoys, nor has he been flashy enough to land on Oprah's list of favorites, Zacharias has had tremendous success impacting millions of people in their pursuit of truth. But what puzzles him most is the romanticizing of it all. The West's infatuation with all things Eastern is ironic, Zacharias says, given the wealth and freedom the West has enjoyed. The East, on the other hand, where Zacharias grew up, has been fraught with poverty, famine, war, and oppression. But even more puzzling to Zacharias is the claim that Christianity is a Western religion when it originated in the heart of the Middle East. Jesus wasn't born in New Jersey, though the trappings some have foisted upon the Christian faith can make it look as if he was.

Some people welcome the idea of finding everything we need inside ourselves. But when I reach into my "internal consciousness" and my "fundamental reality," I don't levitate. Instead, I discover the need for something greater than myself, and I'm always relieved when I remember where to look.

Truth

Truth may not be trendy, but it is a game changer. It's amazing to have something sturdy to hang on to in life, especially when we're slipping.

I've never been the kind of person who assumes others are wrong because they don't agree with me. On the contrary, I've always wanted to know how they came to their conclusion. I've wanted to know what I'm missing. As a follower of Jesus, I'm constantly drawn to the conversations of skeptics and atheists. I read their commentaries and listen to their debates. I've even agreed with them on more than one occasion, such as during one of my stinging losses. I needed someplace to focus my wounded energy. I needed someone to blame. I needed someone to forgive. But each time I ran through my list of potential suspects, I found myself coming up short. I knew that every person I had the right to be angry with had his or her own set of struggles to deal with. So, with no one left to blame, I watched my anger slowly morph into despair.

Then one day it dawned on me who I was actually angry with. God could have kept things from spiraling out of control, but He didn't. And now I was bitter and left with one very troubling question: How do you forgive the Author of forgiveness?

Being mad at God is one of the most unsatisfying activities I can think of. It's like screaming for help with no voice or attempting to swim without arms or legs. It's hard enough to grieve a loss or face the failure of a dream. But finding a place to process the pain when there are no easy answers makes everything worse.

Years ago, when I first learned about some of the songwriters of the Psalms, one of them really stuck with me. Though he lived several thousand years ago, the writer of Psalm 73 seemed to share my pain. He, too, was angry at

God and disillusioned with life. He had tried to be the good guy and follow the rules, but life seemed out of balance to him. The "good" God he'd trusted had let him down, and he wondered why the "bad" people seemed to be doing so much better than him. He wrote: "But as for me, my feet had almost stumbled, my steps had nearly slipped. For I was envious of the arrogant when I saw the prosperity of the wicked" (Psalm 73:2-3 ESV).

Whatever pain the psalmist was experiencing, bitterness was tugging at his heart. Why did he even bother to obey God? What was it all for? "In vain have I kept my heart clean and washed my hands in innocence" (Psalm 73:13 ESV).

The writer's pain became so overwhelming, he began distancing himself from God. And in that hollow space, he didn't like the person he was becoming. "When my soul was embittered, when I was pricked in heart, I was brutish and ignorant; I was like a beast toward you" (Psalm 73:21-22 ESV).

Then, something incredible happened. Amid his anger and disillusionment, the psalmist had a moment of clarity. It was like the moment of clarity King Nebuchadnezzar had in Daniel chapter 4. Nebuchadnezzar had his own brush with insanity when he tried to control things God never asked him to. He too became like a wild beast, until he paused and looked heavenward. Only then could he say, "My reason returned to me" (Daniel 4:34 ESV).

Like Nebuchadnezzar, the psalmist struggled for control too. He wanted his life boxed up neatly. But it wasn't until he humbled himself and forced himself to do the last thing any depressed person wants to do—worship God—that he gained his footing again. "When I thought how to understand this, it seemed to me a wearisome task, until I went into the sanctuary of God" (Psalm 73:16-17 ESV).

In the presence of God, the songwriter gained a fresh perspective. Only then was he able to consider the possibilities of God's sovereign or ultimate control and how He's able to weave together the purposes of our pleasure and pain. "My flesh and my heart may fail, but God is the strength of my heart and my portion forever" (Psalm 73:26 ESV).

When we face disappointment, we really only have two choices. We can turn toward God or we can turn away. We can claim His presence, or we can reject Him altogether. I've watched plenty of people choose the latter because it's easier to believe God isn't there than that He doesn't care. But I've also seen how this becomes the breeding ground for doubt, one of our greatest sources of discontent.

Otherworldly

Paul points out the differences between the spiritual and the physical, even as he acknowledges how they are the same. It may *feel* like it, he tells us in Ephesians 6:12, but our struggles aren't just against "flesh and blood." They're not just against annoying coworkers, mounting credit card debt, or jeans that keep getting tighter. Psychologists tell us that these "issues" are symptoms of a deeper struggle. Why can't we get along with people? Why do we overspend? Why does our dryer keep shrinking our jeans?

Clearly, the fault is not always ours. Sometimes it is the dryer. But if we're part of the problem, we need to know. Even if it's just a matter of learning how to respond better to our issues. Psychologists tell us to go deep, and Paul tells us the same thing. In fact, Paul tells us to go even deeper by pointing out that our struggle isn't merely against "flesh and blood." It's against the "rulers, the authorities, and the powers of this dark world and . . . the spiritual forces of evil in the heavenly realms."

Now, I'll admit, this does sound a little eerie and other-worldly, but I think it's so normal that we hardly even notice it . . . until things tank, that is. In this way I think our discontentment can become a useful marker. It can be an indication of how we're doing in our spiritual life, which makes sense. God doesn't really want us to be content without Him. We were created with a space that only He can fill.

Discontentment can remind us we're veering off course.

Discontentment can remind us we're veering off course. We get so used to seeing things that we hardly notice how incredible they really are. Take childbirth, for example. Having a baby for the first time is amazing, but can it technically be classified as a miracle?

Some people throw that term around so much that it's lost its impact. According to UNICEF, in 2014, approximately 255 babies were born globally every minute. Something this common can hardly be considered a miracle, which is defined as not only a divine intervention but also an *unusual* event. But when you're pregnant for the first time, it seems incredibly unusual. In fact, I was a little freaked out to think I was growing a little humanoid inside of me. But maybe that's just me. Anxiety Girl strikes again.

As a culture, we're pretty sophisticated. In fact, we're so self-sufficient that some of us have even lulled ourselves into believing there's no need for a Creator. Life is about hard work, luck, or fate. There's no more to life than meets the eye.

In Our Stars

Most of us are captivated by the idea of luck. Even if we believe in hard work, good choices, or fate, the phenomenon of coincidence grabs our attention because we want to know why things work out the way they do.

Shankar Vedantam is an American journalist and science correspondent who shares my fascination with how the brain works. He hosts NPR's *Hidden Brain* podcast and recently talked about how coincidence captures our imagination. Vedantam invited his listeners to share their own stories of coincidence, and my favorite was told by a woman who'd studied in Paris. While in Paris, she met someone at a party and discovered that person actually lived in her dad's childhood home in Poughkeepsie, New York.

Amazing, right? Well, leave it to a mathematician to throw a wet blanket on things. Facts and figures can be so inflexible. In his book, *Fluke: The Math and Myth of Coincidence*, Joseph Mazur doubts that coincidences are as significant as we might want them to be, especially when we do the math. Mazur says, "People think that their address book is essentially the people they know, and it turns out any address book is about 1 percent of the people they know in some way."[4]

One of my biggest coincidence stories happened in high school when I had a dream that a classmate named John died. When I got to school the next morning, I learned John hadn't died. Instead, another student I didn't know named Ed was killed in a car accident the night before. Strangely, John didn't go by his first name. He went by his nickname, Ed.

These kinds of incidences can be disturbing on all sorts of levels, but they always set me thinking about "random" events. Fortunately, not all coincidences are painful. And depending on their personality type, I think some people can become quite enamored by a coincidence, particularly when it's cheerful. Who doesn't like a good lottery-winner story?

Vedantam told the story of a woman named Joan Ginther who won the lottery (count 'em) four times. When Vedantam asked Mazur about Ginther's luck, he calculated the odds at about eighteen septillion to one, which is a 1 followed by twenty-four zeros. But if you reframe the question and calculate the odds that *anyone*—not just Joan Ginther—will win the lottery four times, you get much better odds: five million to one. This considers the number of people playing and the fact that most winners use their "house money" to play again, thus further increasing their odds of repeating a win.

Several years ago, at my nephew's wedding reception, they had placed a lottery ticket on each place setting, which was a fun gesture tucked inside a day full of elegance. But what amused me most was my mom's reaction. She's never purchased a lottery ticket in her life. She's far too sensible for that and, technically, doesn't really believe in luck. But there she was, furiously scratching off the numbers, then wondering if she could take the tickets sitting on the plates of the no-shows at the end of the table.

What does it take to win the lottery? Luck? Fate? It is true that you can't win unless you play. But are the odds of winning the lottery—or winning at anything else in life—really worth the risk? That's something everyone must process for themselves as they weigh their options. In business, we call it "risk management." In life, Brené Brown calls it "daring greatly."

I've chipped away at this for a lot of years, and I've concluded that life is a bit of science and statistics mixed together. But the One who holds everything in balance is the One who offers us our greatest hope. Because, at the end of the day, the reliability of cold hard numbers can only take us so far. My mom would tell you this is because no matter how random life feels, in the end, our days were numbered before one of them came to be.

This may sound a little abstract and otherworldly, particularly when we're in a hyper-rational state of mind. But maybe life progresses so naturally, we hardly notice God's involvement or tap into it . . . until things tank, that is. That's when we find ourselves reaching for something more, like George Costanza on *Seinfeld*. When he told Jerry that God was punishing him, Jerry reminded him he didn't believe in God. But George said, "I do for the bad stuff."

Sound familiar? Well, good luck with that.

Chapter Eight

MAKING
FEAR
WORK

I remember sitting in church as a kid and our pastor explaining how spiritual concepts fit into our physical world. He was a great storyteller and was always able to pull my attention away from playing tic-tac-toe on the back of the bulletin with my sister.

He told the story of a woman who struggled with serious credit card debt and couldn't resist a bargain. She knew she needed help. One day she went to see her pastor who said her problem was ultimately a spiritual one. He told her that the next time she was tempted to buy something she didn't really need, she should say out loud, "Get thee behind me, Satan!"

Soon she was drawn to her favorite boutique again and spotted an adorable dress. She thought, "What's the harm in just trying it on?" As she admired her reflection in the fitting room mirror, she felt herself overcome with guilt. She knew she didn't need another dress, but here she was, faced with another temptation. Quickly she remembered her pastor's advice. She looked straight into the mirror and said, "Get thee behind me, Satan!"

Suddenly, a low voice answered back, "The dress looks great from back here too."

Obsessing over evil and looking for it everywhere isn't exactly healthy. But ignoring it altogether can be dangerous too.

This story has stuck with me because it illustrates the subtleties of our spiritual battle and how it directly impacts our deepest sense of contentment. Whatever "the enemy" looks like, Scripture tells us evil often shows up looking good. As "an angel of light," we're told (2 Corinthians 11:14). He's dressed to kill. If he wasn't, we wouldn't need a warning. It's the subtleties that lead to trouble. It's the moment we compromise and ask, "What's the harm in just trying it on?"

Obsessing over evil and looking for it everywhere isn't exactly healthy. But ignoring it altogether can be dangerous too. Kevin Spacey's character in *The Usual Suspects* beautifully paraphrased Charles Baudelaire's provocative quote,

"The greatest trick the Devil ever pulled was convincing the world he didn't exist."

Each of us need to know where we're most vulnerable. What temptations consistently pull us off track? Sex? alcohol? food? spending? Once we make that determination, then we can begin to put up safeguards and draw from the spiritual reserves God offers.

My struggle with fear has been epic, and the enemy has capitalized on it. But I'm constantly amazed at how when I'm veering off-course, simply putting these principles into practice straightens me out . . . *every single time*. What it always boils down to is just how long I want to squirm and struggle before I decide to set things right. Because, again, connecting with God and tapping into His power source is ultimately a choice.

And fear is a crazy entity. Like most things, it's an important part of our lives and useful in many ways. When it warns us of danger, it's a good thing. But when it gets blown out of proportion, it's paralyzing. In college I remember studying the statistics of fear and life stressors in one of my psych classes. Most of us were typical, stressed-out college kids worrying about finals, friends, and our future, so we paid attention. But for me, it was different.

I'd recently been noticing some disturbing symptoms, like strange thoughts, a faster-than-normal pulse, cold hands, and a dry mouth. But back then, I wouldn't have known how to label them as anxiety. And I certainly had no idea I was edging toward a cliff that was about to plunge me into a full-fledged panic disorder. I only knew I'd begun responding to stress in ways that seemed over-the-top. So, when the professor pulled out the list, I really leaned in.

Interestingly, public speaking was ranked as the number-one fear, with our fear of death coming in a close second. Which means, as Jerry Seinfeld says, we're probably better off lying *in* the casket than having to give the eulogy.

Panic Attacks and Public Speaking

Sometimes even I have a hard time believing I stand up in front of people and speak. But my speaking has become the picture of God's work in my life. He offers a power infusion where I need it most. How else could I do it? I am a walking, talking example of God's empowerment. Fear and doubt are what I bring to the table. But, amazingly, God accepts the feeble attempts at faith I offer Him and uses them to perfect His strength in my weakness. That's what He does, as Paul tells us in 2 Corinthians 12:8.

In some ways, as a speaker, I have "fear" to thank for making it "easier" for me to focus on God. Going it alone was never an option . . . unless I wanted to provide some serious drama from the podium. (I probably would have had to charge extra for that bit of entertainment.)

When I first started speaking, I belonged to a group at my church that included lots of older women. There were other groups for young moms like me to choose from, but I sought out the gray-haired set. I understood the wisdom of the whole Titus 2 mentoring thing, and I already had friends my age. Instinctively, I knew I'd learn more from the older women.

But some of them were really old, and the last thing I wanted to do was traumatize them. I was *reeeally* nervous the first time I spoke in front of them. What if I fainted or freaked out at the podium and sent a few of them into cardiac arrest? Crazy as it sounds, even though I was a nervous wreck, I still knew I was "supposed" to speak, even if I made a fool of myself and we had to call 9-1-1. And since doing the right thing has never been about looking good or feeling good, I pushed past my fears and left the details to God.

We can't control everything, and guess what? God never asks us to. We can only do our best and leave Him with the rest. If my obedience meant traumatizing a few women, I figured it would be His responsibility, not mine. I could only do what I was called to do.

Ah, the sweet liberation of God's mysterious sovereignty.

I've learned that even amid fear there can be contentment. We can't protect our kids from every danger, we can't control our spouses, and even our careers can only be controlled to a point. But Scripture tells us that God is in charge, and when difficult things happen, He has promised to walk us through it and meet our most pressing needs.

Billy Graham was asked how he prepared for the thousands of speeches he gave to packed stadiums. He said he prepared as if everything depended on him and then prayed as if everything depended on God. Then he stepped out in faith. That is what I call the perfect balance. That's the fertile soil that allows contentment to grow, even along a thorny path.

Interestingly, many years later, I happened to run into one of the gray-haired women I'd spoken to years before. She was just as vibrant as I remembered, and I realized she probably wasn't quite as old as I'd thought she was when I was in my twenties.

That's the fertile soil that allows contentment to grow, even along a thorny path.

I confessed to her how frightened I was the first time I spoke in front of the ladies and how afraid I was of falling over in front of them. But she just smiled, shrugged her shoulders, and said, "Well, if you had fallen over, we would have just picked you up."

Yes, of course they would have. What did I think would have happened?

The woman had no idea how those few simple words would stick with me and shape my thinking. Why ruin a good day expecting the worst? If it happens, which it probably won't, you'll deal with it through God's grace. But how much more joyful will your day be if instead of obsessing over the worst, you create space for the best?

Fear is normal. Finding ways to deal with it effectively is

essential. I've often thought about how fortunate I was to be surrounded by women who cared about me and wanted me to succeed. But we don't always have that luxury. Sometimes we're not greeted by a welcoming committee. We're forced to walk into the lions' den instead . . . the boardroom, the courtroom, the hospital room. So, we need to plan ahead. Preparing for the difficult times ahead is important. Aligning ourselves with mentors, coaches, and trainers we trust will make all the difference. Even God has gone to extraordinary lengths to invite us to draw on His strength. Which is not to say we'll never struggle.

The Spiritual Side of Taking Risks

Corporate leaders know that risk-taking is the name of the game. It's become synonymous with entrepreneurship.

Mark A. Smith, in his article, "Intolerance, Leadership and Risk-Taking," says business writer Seth Godin is all about taking healthy risks. According to Smith, Godin believes "playing it safe and not taking a risk is probably the most dangerous thing you could do in today's rapidly changing and highly competitive business environment."[1]

Studies point to several factors that cause some people to take risks and others to avoid them, including temperament, experiences, and even cortisol levels. And let's face it, it's easier to take risks when there's not a lot at stake. Or if there's a backup plan to pay the mortgage.

Success stories sell books, but I've found that many of them neglect to tell us the "rest of the story." When I discover an author who's barely out of his or her thirties telling me he or she has made it, I wish them well, then hope they've fastened their seatbelt. Success stories can leave us with the impression that struggling means failure, or that once we've achieved our goal, it'll be smooth sailing. But in the real world, this just isn't true.

I'm an unlikely risk-taker, having struggled for thirteen years with a panic disorder that was fueled by an undiagnosed heart condition. As I mentioned, when I was finally diagnosed and treated, I was more than happy to play things safe. I took my seat in the boat and floated comfortably downstream. But as I grew stronger, I became increasingly uncomfortable with life passing me by. That's when I knew it was time to get out of the boat and take a risk. And it was a big one. To pursue public speaking after years of panic attacks is no small task. That is, of course, unless you're convinced of your calling.

Michael Lewis, author of *The Big Short*, makes the distinction between a job and a calling in life: "A job will never satisfy you all by itself, but it will afford you security and the chance to pursue an exciting and fulfilling life outside your work. A calling is an activity you find so compelling that you wind up organizing your entire self around it."[2]

But a calling doesn't mean an easy ride. Even now, after all these years of speaking, sometimes I still get nervous before an event. I know I'm doing the right thing, but I wonder why doing the right thing isn't easier. Self-doubt kicks in, and my mind races to come up with all sorts of reasons why I'm *not* cut out to be a speaker. I'll wonder how I got myself into this mess and come up with creative reasons to cancel. *I could give myself food poisoning*, I think, as I help myself to another scoop of raw cookie dough. *I could scream really loud and lose my voice as I did when the Packers won their last Super Bowl.* (The group I spoke to the next day was mighty gracious, given the fact I was in Bears' territory.)

And none of this is ever made easier when I start thinking about the coordinators of the event, who are probably on edge as much as I am. Their team has been planning for more than a year, and they're counting on me. *Ugh.*

This is when the abstract concept of "spiritual warfare" becomes real to me. Most of us read Paul's spiritually charged words in Ephesians 6:10-20 and think, *Yeah, good for him. But I live in the real world.* Whatever good and evil looks like, the struggle between taking the easy way out and doing the right thing can get very intense. And all I can say after all these years is that being on the winning side makes all the difference.

After being yanked around a bit, I'll gather up my notes and make my way to the podium knowing my faith will be restored. It always is. I'll watch this frightened girl transform into a confident speaker once again and see the power of calling at work.

Confidence comes from being true to your calling. It makes abstract phrases concrete, such as, "God's strength is made perfect in our weakness." These are the words the apostle Paul used when he spoke about a mysterious affliction he called a "thorn in the flesh." Scholars like to speculate about the thorn Paul mentions in 2 Corinthians 12:1-10. Was it malaria, migraines, or Paul's ongoing problem with his eyes? I think the answer was left blank intentionally, so we could fill it with our own thorn: Work. Family. Health. Finances.

Clearly my panic disorder was my thorn in the flesh, and my ability to speak is God's strength made perfect in my weakness. Knowing our calling, whatever it is, enables us to press through the tough times. Because they will come. And, the fact is, it's much easier to find a comfortable seat in the boat and just plant ourselves there. There's nothing risky about being a spectator. But I've become convinced that most of us can accomplish far more than we think, if we're willing to take a risk. We just need to discover our calling, lean over the side of the boat, and dip our toe into the water.

Confidence comes from being true to your calling.

Spiritual Self-Control

Every time I speak, I'm reminded of what we can accomplish when we step outside our comfort zone and trust God.

That's true even when it's baptism by fire, as was the case for me in the early days of my speaking.

The first two rules you learn about public speaking are (1) know your audience and (2) know your material. But I was brand new to the game when I agreed to speak at a banquet in downtown Milwaukee, so what did I know? The coordinator who booked me must have been a newbie too, because she overlooked rule number one by neglecting to share with me one very important detail about her women. And the rude awakening I was about to get would teach me never to neglect rule number one again.

So, in my blissful naiveté, I set out to prepare my talk. Jill Briscoe, my mentor at the time, had taught me four steps when preparing a talk with spiritual underpinnings: pray about the topic, study what the Scriptures have to say about it, read other material and educate yourself, and keep your eyes open.

The coordinator had told me the women had been discussing Galatians 5 and the "fruit of God's spirit," as the apostle Paul called it. She wanted me to talk specifically about our struggle with self-control. And again, speaking from experience, I knew I'd have more material than I needed. The apostle Paul tackles another area of life that can become a nasty threat to our sense of contentment: the lack of self-control. He begins by pointing out the obvious, namely, that we can expect to find a virtual cornucopia of self-control challenges in this world. According to Paul, they include "sexual immorality, impurity and debauchery; idolatry and witchcraft; hatred, discord, jealousy, fits of rage, selfish ambition, dissensions, factions and envy; drunkenness, orgies, and the like" (Galatians 5:19-21).

Did he leave anything out?

Even the good things in life that bring us pleasure can destroy us if indulged in excess. And why one person can be satisfied with a little whereas another believes that a lot is a whole lot better remains somewhat of a mystery. Brain chemicals, learned patterns of behavior, and coping mechanisms, all contribute to the challenge. But, in the end, self-control begins with the decision to be self-controlled. When we recognize the power of self-control and learn how to walk through life equipped to respond effectively to even our greatest temptations, our lives will be different. They will become empowered. But it begins with a choice.

We can train ourselves to be self-controlled. Athletes do it all the time. And it's not as though we can never be successful or happy in life if we choose to go it without God. There's a measure of pleasure in life for everyone to enjoy. A sunrise. A hug. A taste bud. Even atheists who reject God have been so insulated by His blessings they don't even see them. The Book of Matthew tells us it rains "on the just and the unjust" (5:45 ESV). But Paul points out that if we want to take everything to the next level, that option is available.

I was fully prepared to give my talk when the day of

the banquet finally arrived. So, I headed into the city, found a place to park, and walked into the beautifully gentrified brick building. I noticed several women putting finishing touches on their festive tables. But other than that, the enormous room was empty.

One of the event planners approached me with a welcoming smile. She could see the confusion on my face as I looked at the rows of empty chairs, so she said, "The buses should be arriving any minute."

"Buses?" I asked her.

"Yes," she said. "Didn't they tell you the women will be coming from prison and halfway houses?"

"No," I answered. "I guess they forgot."

Seeing the color drain from my face, the woman tried to assure me. "Everything will be fine," she said. "The women will love you."

But I wasn't so sure. Why would the women love me? They'd take one look at me, this blonde girl from the suburbs, and wonder what I could possibly know of their struggle.

Then, as if I wasn't rattled enough, the woman added, "I should warn you, though. Sometimes the audience can be a little rude. They've been known to yell things out at the speaker. But don't let that throw you!" She quickly added, "Just keep going. You'll be fine."

I nodded slowly and suddenly noticed how warm the room felt. Droplets of sweat gathered along my back as

I watched the women file in. They looked like a serious bunch, I thought, as the full irony of the situation suddenly hit me. I was about to give a talk on the topic of self-control to women who were straight out of prison. An obvious struggle for all of them.

I found a chair in the corner of the room and began scribbling furiously at my notes. This joke was no longer funny. That line was no longer appropriate. Soon, another coordinator spotted me. Sensing my desperation, she walked over and asked if I'd like the committee to pray for me. It was an offer I couldn't refuse.

The banquet had been organized by a group of Pentecostal women who were doing fabulous work in the inner city. The women led me to a door in the back of the hall, and when we stepped inside, I realized that it was a broom closet. The door closed behind us, and everything went black. I suddenly felt several sets of hands land on my head and my shoulders as the women began praying as though there was no tomorrow, which I suddenly wished there wasn't. I'd heard of "prayer closets" before, but I never knew they actually included mops and buckets.

I couldn't understand a word they were saying as they spoke in various tongues. But as we stepped out of the closet and back into the light, it was reassuring to know God understood every heart. *Let the power infusion begin!*

As I grabbed my notes and made the exceptionally long walk to the podium, I was suddenly reminded of why I was there. The women attending the banquet weren't there to be entertained by me. They had come to hear truth that sets the prisoner free. "He has sent me to bind up the broken-hearted, to proclaim freedom for the captives" (Isaiah 61:1).

I reminded the women that we all struggle with self-control issues. Some of them are impossible to hide, but others are neatly tucked away in lives that look extremely tidy. But if we're honest with ourselves, we can all identify things that keep us from reaching our potential. Jesus offers a solution. He tells us that when we learn how to access God's power through the simple spiritual disciplines of prayer and meditation, our lives will change.

You could have heard a pin drop.

A God Complex

Allowing God to speak to us through His word may not sound very flashy, but it's incredibly powerful. And though He can speak to us in several ways, it remains His top mode of communication. In fact, He went to great lengths to make that happen, utilizing more than forty authors and one thousand years.

He could have chosen to leave us to our own devices, trying to read nature and interpret

Allowing God to speak to us through His word may not sound very flashy, but it's incredibly powerful.

circumstances, as the deists would claim. But I believe He initiated dialogue. Why wouldn't He?

Hearing from God, through His word, and learning how to yield to His spirit is exactly how we tap into our own life's potential. It's also how we influence others. Though, ultimately, as much as we may want to, only God can change a heart.

I had a friend who was growing annoyed with her fiancé. He was a brand-new Christian and *on fire*, as they say! It's easy to understand why a person who discovers grace should be excited. The problem arises when the newly enlightened becomes so excited they annoy everyone around them, as my friend's fiancé did. Instead of focusing on his own relationship with God, he was all about "fixing" hers. She told him she believed, but that wasn't enough. He needed more evidence. So, instead of letting her journey progress in its own way, he decided to take on the role of the Holy Spirit himself.

One night, he decided to take her out for dinner and use the opportunity to set her straight. But by the time their meal was over, she was so annoyed with him, they hardly spoke. She headed to the restroom while he picked up the check, and as he pulled out his wallet, a stranger approached him. He gently put his hand on the fiancé's shoulder and confessed that he'd been sitting in the next booth listening to their entire conversation. Then the stranger looked into his eyes, smiled, and said, "My friend, you plant the seeds, but let the Lord bring in the harvest." Then he walked away.

My friend's story was very cool. And I have to say, it did give a little credence to the idea of "entertaining angels unaware." The stranger's advice was good for the young zealot who needed to take it down a notch. But it was also good for anyone who's tempted to take on a project only God is qualified to do, in their own lives or in the lives of others. Living with a messiah complex can put a serious strain on anyone.

Accessing God's power through humility may sound uber-simplistic, but for many of us, it's an ongoing battle. We like feeling in control, and that tends to make humility a bit of a challenge.

When Atheists Smile

Pride can be a tricky thing. For example, too much humility can be another form of pride, as when we're too proud to accept someone's help. Plus, right about the time we think we've got the pride thing licked, well, that's probably just our pride talking. Writing a book on doubt introduced me to lots of brilliant minds who were quite full of themselves. Maybe I'd have the same problem if I were that brilliant. No worries there.

Thomas Nagel is a renowned professor of philosophy at New York University. Born in Yugoslavia to a Jewish family, he began publishing philosophy at the ripe old age of twenty-two. Fifty years later, he's written extensively on how the human mind has been shaped by modern science. In his book, *Mind and Cosmos*, Nagel, an atheist, talks about his inability to see God. Analytic philosopher Alvin Plantinga "sadly" quotes Nagel as saying, "I lack the *sensus divinitatis* [sense of divinity] that enables—indeed compels—so many people to see in the world the expression of divine purpose as naturally as they see in a smiling face the expression of human feeling."[3]

Nagel was responding to a statement made by French theologian John Calvin five hundred years ago. Calvin wrote "that there exists in the human mind and indeed by natural instinct, some sense of Deity [*sensus divinitatis*], we hold to be beyond dispute, since God himself, to prevent any man from pretending ignorance, has endued all men with some idea of his Godhead. . . . This is not a doctrine which is first learned at school, but one as to which every man is, from the womb, his own master; one which nature herself allows no individual to forget."[4]

Calvin, who obviously shared the apostle Paul's tendency toward run-on sentences, was echoing Paul's insights found in his letter to the church in Rome. Paul points out that every one of us is born with some awareness of God through both creation and conscience. Creation simply means that when we see a sunset or the birth of a baby, we know there's something bigger than ourselves. And conscience is that thing inside us that tells us it's wrong to shove an old lady off the sidewalk and take her purse. C. S. Lewis refers to this as a clue to the universe. However, individuals who have thought clearly, with their freedom of choice, mind you, may yet choose to snuff out the flicker of God's flame burning inside of them.

These two concepts are the reason Paul could make the bold statement, "People are without excuse" (Romans 1:20). God can and will judge fairly all people, whether they've heard the name of Jesus or not. As Immanuel Kant said, "Two things fill the mind with ever new and increasing admiration and awe, the more often and steadily we reflect upon them: the starry heavens above me and the moral law within me."[5]

Nagel is an interesting guy and distinguishes himself from some of his more rabid atheist contemporaries. Though he resists a "religious" framework, Nagel says the idea that complex life originated purely by accident flies in the face of common sense. "Where does rationality fit in?" he wonders.

Nagel says a teleological argument is far more logical than a purely materialistic one. Something of purpose must account for the complexities of life, he points out, particularly conscious life—though Nagel stops short of offering ideas as to what that "something" might be.

I'm always fascinated by discussions about the relationship between science and faith. In an interview with Oxford professor John Lennox, a personal hero of mine, along with Francis Collins and others, Lennox said that although people have always lived in varying degrees of enlightenment, this militant new atheism we hear about is a contemporary concept. It's a complete preoccupation with self-aggrandizement. Lennox points out that when Sir Isaac Newton discovered the law of gravity, he didn't say, "How brilliant am I?" Instead, he said, "How brilliant is the God I'm discovering." There's never been a contest between science and faith, Lennox says. "God no more competes with science as an explanation for the universe than Henry Ford competes with the law of internal combustion as an explanation for the motor car. You don't choose between Henry Ford and the automobile any more than you choose between God and science."[6]

C. S. Lewis believed people became scientists because they believed in the law of science and a lawgiver. There is rationality and mathematic intelligibility behind the universe that compels men and women of science forward, says Lennox, a professor of mathematics himself. But hubris in science, which is fancy talk for excessive pride, is a dangerous commodity. Actually, hubris in anything is a dangerous commodity if it keeps us from seeing our need. That's what Jesus meant when he said, "It is easier for a camel to go through the eye of a needle than for someone who is rich to enter the kingdom of God" (Matthew 19:24).

Scholars like to debate whether Jesus meant an actual sewing needle or a small gateway that existed back in his day that a camel couldn't fit through. Either way, the meaning is the same. The more self-sufficient people become, the more they begin to believe their own press. Whether through riches or brilliance, God gets edged out. But again, I don't see this happening to me any time soon.

And I'm not referring to self-confidence or self-respect. That's important. What I am talking about is the mind-set that somehow scientific advancement is competing with the concept of God, which it is not. It never has, and it never will. Every scientific discovery we make is about discovering more about the wonder of God and His creative power. That's what puts a smile on His face.

Chapter Nine

WHAT CAN YOU OFFER?

II. Body (offer our bodies)

These days it's much trendier to be called "spiritual" rather than "religious." But just give it time. It seems like every generation has its own list of "acceptable" and "unacceptable" terms. (Eye roll.) Either way, surveys consistently indicate that most people agree with spiritual concepts . . . at least in theory. This is because we're hardwired for something more, an empty space God desires to fill.

Spiritually speaking, it's easy to get fired up by a good sermon or a seminar that stimulates all sorts of ideas for self-improvement. And, doggone it, we mean it! We want to be kinder, more honest, and more generous. The problem starts when we leave the conference or the sanctuary and head back home to the "real" world. The moment we walk in the door, the spiritual issues of life are no longer abstract. Relationships are strained, bills need to be paid, and suddenly we don't feel quite as confident as we did only hours before. This is when things get dicey. Which is why Jesus said, "The spirit is willing, but the flesh is weak" (Matthew 26:41).

> We're hardwired for something more, an empty space God desires to fill.

In Romans 12:1, the apostle Paul says our spiritual act of worship is to offer our *bodies* "as a living sacrifice." But most of us haven't a clue what that really means. And if we have any ideas about what a "sacrifice" might look like, whether from Stephen King books or horror movies, we can get creeped out pretty quickly. Particularly if we hear the term "blood" sacrifice. *Eww.*

The idea of bloodshed is troubling enough, but a bird or a little lamb offered as a sacrifice? *Yuck.* What could be more disturbing to our modern-day PETA thinking? So, let me offer a little perspective. For starters, I love animals as much as the next guy. I have zero tolerance for any kind of abuse or suffering. But sometimes even I wonder if as a culture we haven't gotten just a bit extreme with our animal devotion. We were brought up on Bambi and Nemo. And we're pretty sure that when we're not looking, wild animals are in their little forest houses setting tables for tea and discussing the weather. *"Tut, tut."*

We don't even see our animals as pets anymore. They're family members, which I totally get. My bloodhound was as spoiled as any family member could ever be. Some of us don't even like to acknowledge animals as a source of sustenance. If we had to pluck feathers as our great grandparents did, we'd probably all starve. And even if we're not completely vegan, most of us don't want to know how the cordon bleu got on our plates. It just magically appears with the rice pilaf, right?

Of course, not everyone feels this way about animals. My mom thinks the whole "pet reverence" thing is out of control. According to her, it's a perfect example of Romans 1:25, when Paul warns us not to worship the created more than the Creator. She grew up on a farm where chickens were for dinner and dogs and cats slept in the barn. It's not that she dislikes animals or wishes them harm, she just can't understand how entire work schedules and vacation plans are adjusted to accommodate a pet. And the vet bills? Don't *even* get her started. I shouldn't have mentioned the sign in the vet's office reminding us to bring our pets in for their "six-month wellness" checkup. I don't even do that for myself.

Sometimes I think my mom has a point, especially when I'm scooping up poop while she's lounging on the deck. But I ask you, who else breaks into a happy dance the minute I walk in the door after taking out the garbage?

Maybe I am needier than Mom is. Heaven knows I

enjoy the love of a snuggly puppy. And my English mastiffs embodied the prayer, "Lord, make me the kind of person my dog thinks I am."

A Living Sacrifice

All this to say that the idea of offering any kind of animal sacrifice couldn't be more distasteful to our twenty-first-century sensibilities. But because scriptural truths are meant to transcend time and culture, engaging some good "hermeneutics" skills when we read the Bible (aka biblical interpretation tools) is essential.

To avoid confusion, whenever we read any portion of Scripture, we need to ask four questions:

1. Who said it?
2. Who did they say it to?
3. What did it mean to them?
4. What does it mean to us?

There's always a nugget of truth we can learn from any passage of Scripture. Understanding how to interpret it makes all the difference. For example, just knowing whether the passage is meant to be taken literally or figuratively can keep us from getting all mixed up.

Darrell Bock is a New Testament scholar who uses a football analogy to highlight the importance of solid hermeneutics. If he said, "The Cheeseheads murdered the Monsters of the Midway on The Frozen Tundra," most people in our culture, particularly NFL fans, would know that no arrest warrants would be necessary and that the Green Bay Packers had defeated the Chicago Bears at Lambeau Field.

A long view of the Old Testament, and some solid hermeneutics, can help us understand the significance of the sacrificial system. From the beginning of recorded history, it was meant to teach us something significant about the Lifegiver and His flawless nature.

A Step Back in Time

By the time the Book of Leviticus was written, a book that's filled with troubling imagery if not interpreted properly, God's people were familiar with the entire sacrificial system. They also understood the significance of each offering. The five main types were the burnt offering, the grain offering, the peace offering, the sin offering, and the trespass offering.

The burnt offering was an act of worship and a way of asking God's forgiveness for offenses committed unintentionally. The grain offering came from the fields and expressed a thankful heart for a good harvest and other blessings. The peace offering was similar and included animals or grains as a thanksgiving blessing. The trespass offering symbolized cleansing from the defilement of our sin, again, as individuals would compare themselves to God's perfection.

The first three offerings were considered voluntary. But the last two were mandatory, and they involved bloodshed. Why, you ask? There are two reasons.

First, in Leviticus 17, we're reminded that the "life of a creature is in the blood." Blood is what keeps us alive. People understood this concept long before corpuscles were discovered under a microscope, and we found out how cells deliver nutrients to the body. In ancient times, things were much more basic. People could see for themselves that if you bled, you died. So, the powerful imagery of bloodshed illustrated the high cost of sin. It led to death.

> Let's admit it, having freedom of choice doesn't mean we always choose wisely.

Second, the shedding of blood ultimately pointed to Christ. For thousands of years, before Jesus even walked the earth, God's people were becoming familiar with the significance of sacrifice. They'd also been told to watch for the coming Messiah, whom the New Testament Book of Hebrews describes as the "perfect offering" or "the Lamb without blemish." Jesus brought the imagery full circle.

Let's admit it, having freedom of choice doesn't mean we always choose wisely. And God could have given up on us, especially as we've turned our backs on Him. But, amazingly, He didn't, and He doesn't. Nor did He "compromise" His righteousness by simply "overlooking" our sin. Instead, He dealt with the problem of "unrighteousness" head-on, as a perfect father who corrects His child, then gives a second chance . . . and a third, and a fourth. In fancy theological terms, we call that "atonement" for our sins. It means that Jesus paid the penalty for us and fulfilled the high demands of the law. No longer would sacrifices be needed, because Jesus paid the debt in full.

It's like if you're out with friends enjoying drinks and appetizers. The conversation is so good, you hardly notice how quickly the tab starts running up. Then the check comes. You reach for your wallet, but it's not there because you left it on your dresser back home. Remember? You feel a little panicky and embarrassed. Until that one friend, the really rich one who's incredibly generous, picks up the check and says with a smile, "Don't worry. It's my treat."

Yeah, it's like that. Jesus paid a debt that He did not owe because we owed a debt we could not pay.

Back to the Future

By the time the apostle Paul said, in Romans 12:1, that our spiritual act of worship is "to offer your bodies as a living sacrifice," it meant something. By then, his listeners had become extremely familiar with the idea of sacrifice. It acknowledged God's place in their lives. The question is, what do Paul's words mean for us today? I think the answer to this will appear different for everyone. When we look at the creative diversity in our world, why would we assume anything else? Followers of Christ were never called to a "cookie-cutter" faith. Not that there's a problem with that, per se.

Some people are comfortable worshipping with people who look like them, act like them, and sound like them. And that's fine. The problem begins when people start imposing their own "comfort zone" on others, especially when they say it's their way or the highway. We've seen plenty of examples of this in our culture, and the fall-out has been enormous. It's one of the main reasons people steer clear of "organized" religion. But some rules or guidelines are necessary in any society if people want to maintain some semblance of order. A basic understanding of shared expectations avoids chaos in any culture. This is true in the church as well. But there's a big difference between rules that simply keep things running smoothly and rules that are, as theologians put it, "salvific." Rules left to our discretion reflect diversity and should be celebrated as such, not used to destroy each other. But rules that pertain to someone's "salvation" or how an individual will stand before God one day are not arbitrary. They're not based on someone's opinion but rather on the revealed work of Christ.

To offer ourselves as living sacrifices is to embrace the

> *The problem begins when people start imposing their own "comfort zone" on others, especially when they say it's their way or the highway.*

things that bring God pleasure. And how do we know what brings Him pleasure? Again, because He told us. The Old Testament prophet Micah was inspired by God to put it this way: "He has shown you, O mortal, what is good. And what does the LORD require of you? To act justly and to love mercy and to walk humbly with your God" (Micah 6:8).

In the New Testament, James, the leader of the Jerusalem church, says, "Religion that God our Father accepts as pure and faultless is this: to look after orphans and widows in their distress and to keep oneself from being polluted by the world" (James 1:27).

It's that simple . . . or is it?

The Stuff That Holds Us Back . . .

All people have something that trips them up, something that keeps them from being all they could be. We can call it sin, but I've discovered that if we refer to it the way the apostle Paul often did, as a "self-control" issue, it becomes much more tangible. Much more real.

Temptations are a very personalized thing. I can look at a hot bowl of buttered pasta or a freshly mixed strawberry daiquiri and feel nothing. I can appreciate a designer hand-bag or a hunky handyman, and neither tempt me. But open a fresh bag of Ruffles on day two of a diet or put a scoop of ice cream on a slice of chocolate cake, then see what happens. *What diet?*

Everyone has a breaking point, and unless we enjoy our lives spinning out of control on a regular basis, we had better identify the things that can derail us. How content can a person be if one's life is a train wreck?

And before we get all "superior" on folks because they struggle with things we don't, we'd better acknowledge something upfront. People do not come to the table on equal footing. This is true with anything, but particularly with biblical concepts. Fortunately for us, God understands those differences, which is why He doesn't judge us in the same way. Luke 12:48 tells us that to whom much is given, much is required. And like any caring parent, God never frustrates us by setting a goal He isn't willing to help us meet. He knows exactly when to "comfort the afflicted and afflict the comfortable," as the saying goes. So, here's a tip for those who are constantly frustrated. If you're surrounded by religious folk who pressure you to look like them, it may be time to find some new religious folk.

People do not come to the table on equal footing.

My kids are a great example of our built-in differences. They came from the same place, they were brought up in the same environment, yet they were very unalike. I never had to tell my son to keep his room clean, do his homework, or save his money. Somehow, he was always tidy, always more concerned about his schoolwork than I was, and always naturally saving his resources. He was very sensitive to a stern warning.

My daughter, on the other hand, was the opposite. Money burned a hole in her pocket, her room was always a mess, and she was the queen of last-minute Sunday night homework. (That was always fun.) I knew I was in trouble when she was about twenty-two months and *supposed* to be watching TV while I ran upstairs to make beds. Evidently, Mr. Rogers wasn't quite as gripping as I'd hoped, so she decided to create her own entertainment. My son's baseball tee looked interesting to her. The only problem was she couldn't find any whiffle balls. Not that a little detail like that would stop her. She went to the fridge and grabbed the eggs. They provided the perfect trajectory.

When I walked into the family room and saw what she'd done, I wasn't sure whether to laugh or cry. And things only got more interesting from there. At four years old, I scolded her for drawing arrows on the wall with markers. I told her never to do it again, and she didn't. She drew X's on the carpet instead.

I decided to call my mom for support. Was this harmless immaturity or something more diabolical? Her response was classic grandma. She praised my daughter's tenacity and called her a real go-getter! "She'll go far in life," my mom said, "if you don't kill her first."

As a parent, I've tried to remain philosophical about my kids' differences. I figured if I didn't take credit for the one, I couldn't be blamed for the other.

And here's the kicker. I now realize that if I'd only had one child, my son, I could have easily become one of those obnoxious moms, all judgy and blaming parents for their out-of-control kids. But from the day she was born with those gigantic blue eyes casing the joint, my daughter put an end to that. She provided the balance I needed. She taught me what grace means.

My son is a hard worker and excels at everything. He too had to overcome the temptation to judge others too harshly, including his younger sister, for not measuring up to his standards. I've had to remind him that while I appreciate his hard work, his sister has faced more obstacles than he has.

With my daughter, I've had to remind her not to be too hard on herself. When she's tempted to tear herself down, I remind her to give herself a break. I help her recognize how her own struggles have given her a unique sense of empathy. It's easier to appreciate grace when you recognize how much you need it.

The Struggle

Our bodies crave all sorts of things. And if those needs are not being met in healthy ways, they'll try to get met in unhealthy ways. Women tell me all the time the things they wrestle with: smoking, drinking, eating, spending, stealing, cheating, lying, flirting, yelling, criticizing. Not only is the list long and varied, but we seem to have an amazing capacity for rationalizing almost any behavior. As the classic church-lady said when accused of gossip, "What gossip? I was sharing a prayer request."

In seventh grade, my middle school (previously known as junior high) held mock elections. You know, *Best Smile, Most Athletic, Future Principal*. That sort of thing. I was surprised to snag several honors, including *Best Dressed*, which was ironic since I risked my life stealing my sister's clothes every morning. I was also elected *8:25 Champ*, which was fitting since I barely made it to class on time. And I was also elected *Best Excuse Giver*.

In retrospect, my combined honors should have pointed to a future in politics. But when I told my parents about my achievements, they weren't impressed, particularly with the *Best Excuse Giver*. Evidently, I was the kind of kid who liked winning arguments, which drove my parents crazy. More than once I'd hear them say, "Ann, you always have to get the last word in." And I'd say, "No, I don't."

Years later, I came across a quote by Benjamin Franklin that I think is spot-on. He said, "I never knew a man who was good at making excuses who was good at anything else." I agree. I'd also add that being around people who are never wrong is exhausting.

I read an article posted by *More Entertainment* called "Really? The Dumbest Celebrity Excuses for Bad, Bad Behavior." The list includes ten people who have elevated excuse-making to an art form.

1. Tatum O'Neal, arrested for buying crack in 2008: "I bought crack because my dog died."

2. Lindsay Lohan, arrested and searched after a high-speed chase in 2007 (two months after receiving probation for a DUI, I might add): "Someone else left the cocaine in these pants."

3. Newt Gingrich, in 2011, blaming his infidelities on working too hard as a politician: "I cheated on my wife because I love America." (Full disclosure, I searched for the quote, and the closest I got was him saying, "There's no question at times of my life, partially driven by how passionately I felt about this country, that I worked far too hard and things happened in my life that were not appropriate.")

4. Ashlee Simpson, caught lip-synching on SNL in 2004: "I lip-synch because of acid reflux."

5. Charlie Sheen, after trashing a hotel room and threatening a prostitute in 2010: "I had an allergic reaction to medication."

6. George Rekers, caught returning

from a European vacation with a hired male escort in 2010: "He was carrying my luggage."

7. Nicole Richie, caught driving the wrong way on an LA highway in 2006, with marijuana and Vicodin in her system: "I have cramps."

8. Winona Ryder, arrested for shoplifting in Beverly Hills in 2001: "I shoplifted to prepare for a role."

9. Khloe Kardashian, picked up for a DUI in 2007: "I was upset by the anniversary of my father's death."

10. Sylvester Stallone, arrested in 2009 with close to fifty vials of HGH: "The steroids are for a medical condition."

Okay, let's be generous. Maybe there was some truth to these excuses. But this list, though wildly entertaining, does remind us of how good we can get at justifying almost anything.

Keeping It Real

When we think about our self-control issues, we may think about shoving that third brownie into our mouth or freaking out on our nine-year-old for spilling the milk

. . . again. We may think about finishing an entire bottle of wine on our own or lingering too long with an old flame on Facebook . . . a different kind of "online predator." But self-control issues go much deeper than that. Without getting too psychological here, they are an expression of what's *really* going on inside of us. Biblical writers talked about this long before Freud.

_____

Self-control empowers us physically, mentally, and emotionally.

_____

The wisdom literature of the Old Testament warns us to guard our "hearts" (which in Hebrew thought meant our minds and our volition) because everything we do flows from it. Examining this from different angles, the writers said:

> Whoever is slow to anger is better than the mighty,
> and he who rules his spirit than he who takes a city.
> (Proverbs 16:32 ESV)

> "Like a city whose walls are broken through is a person who lacks self-control." (Proverbs 25:28)

Self-control empowers us physically, mentally, and emotionally. It fuels every high-achiever on the planet, like Olympic medalists, CEOs, and stay-at-home moms. Think about it—how many successful people do you know who are completely undisciplined? Business magazines routinely highlight common threads that weave their way through the lives of successful men and women. For many, their personal disciplines extend far beyond their 9-to-5 habits.

Time posted an article in 2015 called "35 Business Leaders Share Their Daily Habits." They included organizational skills, such as clearing out inboxes and unsubscribing from emails. However, there are exceptions to the "tidy" rule. Many believe the notorious clutter of Mark Twain and Albert Einstein merely reflected their creative genius. So, again, you need to do what works for you.

The article also offered time-management tips, such as scheduling meetings close together when your "head is still in the zone." Rest was important, too, along with recreation. Simply spending an hour outside the office walking or riding a bike could make a difference.

When it comes to promoting health, exercise remains at the top of every list, along with kicking the smoking habit. Yet working out is often the first thing to go when we're crunched for time. Especially for caregivers who worry more about everyone around them. Then the next thing you know, another year has gone by and your running shoes are collecting dust in the closet.

I remember one day, after the holidays, when New Year's resolutions were still in full swing, I went to the gym and noticed they were making a real effort to welcome back the prodigals. Posters and articles lined the walls. One of the cartoons that caught my eye was of two guys standing next to each other in their workout gear. One was tall and slender, and the other was short and overweight. The tall one looked down at the short one in disgust and asked, "Don't you have any self-respect? Don't you know your body is a temple?" The short guy answered, "I know my body is a temple. I'm just putting on an addition."

Let's face it, most of us don't expect to win an Olympic medal any time soon, nor will we ever run a Fortune 500 company. But our lives are just as important, and the amount of self-control we harness will be in direct proportion to how successful those lives can become.

The Last Word

I've wrestled with so many self-control issues through the years, it's hard to pick just one as an example. But let's take my need to get the last word in and win an argument, because I'm probably not alone in this. Like so many things, my debating skills can be a two-edged sword. These skills can come in handy for politicians or lawyers, but when someone refuses to see someone else's point of view, they may win the battle but lose the war.

This all became glaringly evident to me years ago when my son was about eight and we were vacationing. One afternoon we walked into a little shop filled with hand-crafted toys. My son walked toward a pile of wooden yo-yos painted brightly red, picked one up, and asked if we could buy it.

I noticed the sign taped to the bin and shook my head. "Too expensive," I said a little too loudly. The toys were clearly overpriced, so I suggested we go home and ask Daddy if he'd cut us a piece of wood. We could file it down ourselves, add some string, paint it red, and it wouldn't cost us a thing. It seemed like a good idea until the woman behind the cash register walked over to where we were standing. She stopped directly in front of us and said, "Excuse me, would you please tell your son to put my merchandise down? You're probably just in here to steal ideas, so I'd like you to leave my store."

Well . . . I'd like to say we left quietly, but we didn't. My first instinct was to defend my innocent little boy, who wasn't hurting a thing. I took the yo-yo from his hand, tossed it back into its bin, and said, "You have no idea why we're in your store."

I grabbed my son's hand and added, "I think your whole attitude is offensive." Then we marched out the door. *Slam dunk*. What an exit! It was strange, though, I thought, as we walked through the parking lot. Where was that good feeling I used to get from winning arguments? Where was that delicious feeling of victory? I'd gotten the last word in, so why was I so uncomfortable? Could my parents have been right? When I got back to the house and told my mom what had happened, her response was, "Oh, those poor shopkeepers. I don't know how they make a living."

Yeah. That's what I needed to hear.

I spent the entire evening haunted by my behavior. I even prayed about it, which is never a good idea if you don't want to hear from God. And to make matters worse, I'd recently studied 1 Corinthians 6, where Paul was speaking to a group of people who obviously shared my problem. Evidently, there were disputes among believers in Corinth. Even back then lawsuits were flying. Paul wrote, "The very fact that you have lawsuits among you means you have been completely defeated already. Why not rather be wronged? Why not rather be cheated? Instead, you yourselves cheat and do wrong, and you do this to your brothers and sisters" (1 Corinthians 6:7-8).

Paul may have been addressing some particular legal action. Not that there isn't a time for that. But he was also putting his finger on a larger issue for the people he was writing to (and for me). It was the perfect example of how God speaks to us through His word. So, again, if you don't want to hear from God, don't read the Bible and don't pray.

I didn't know anything about the shopkeeper. Maybe she was cranky because she was sick. Maybe her husband was leaving her. Maybe she was losing her business. And all I kept thinking was what a breath of fresh air I was *not*. As the evening went on, I grew increasingly uncomfortable, which is always great around bedtime. And what made it worse was that it was becoming increasingly clear what God wanted me to do. Apologize.

I remember looking at the clock and realizing with some relief that the shop was probably closed. *Sorry, Lord. Really.* But the next morning it was like He was standing at the foot of my bed, smiling, and saying, "Good morning! Guess what we're going to do today?" *Ugh.*

I decided to take my son with me. Not only would he be some moral support, but he had witnessed the entire episode the day before. I told him I needed to apologize for being unkind.

Then, I warned him how the woman might respond. "She might freak out on me," I said.

"Cool!" was his answer.

As we drove to town, I reminded myself how it didn't really matter how she responded. I was doing the right thing. Period. I parked the minivan, took my son's hand, and we walked into the shop where the woman spotted us immediately. We locked eyes, so I gave her a little wave and a weak smile.

She walked over to us, and I quickly said, "Hello. Remember me?" She remembered.

Then, before I could say another word, she spoke. She said, "I'm glad you came back. I felt terrible about the way I treated you yesterday."

"No, no!" I answered. "I came here to apologize to you!"

The exchange was brief but very warm. And as my son and I walked out of the shop that day, little red yo-yo in hand, there's only one word to describe the way I felt inside.

Clean. It was the kind of clean that washes so much unhappiness away.

I kept the yo-yo long after my son was done playing with it. In the Old Testament, when people wanted to remember an event, they stacked stones or planted trees. The toy became a visual reminder of what I'd never forget.

Chapter Ten

TAKE BACK CONTROL

The Old Testament Book of Daniel is packed. It contains enough heartwarming stories to keep any Sunday school teacher happy and enough weighty issues to keep scholars debating. I find it fascinating because it provides honest accounts of people who struggled with discontentment, specifically as it relates to struggling for control. Not self-control but God's control, which can be another self-control issue. Their stories remind me that whenever we decide to arm wrestle with God, things don't typically end well for us. Still, we do it anyway, as King Nebuchadnezzar did.

Daniel and his people were captured by King Nebuchadnezzar's Babylon around 580 BC. Daniel was a young prophet at the time and must have been something special, because when the officials were told to evaluate the prisoners and select the "best of the best" to train for the king's service, Daniel was among them.

The young men were to be attractive, "without physical defect, handsome," Daniel 1:4 says. I picture a Zac Efron or a Jake Gyllenhaal. But they also needed to be smart, "showing every kind of aptitude for learning, well-informed, [and] quick to understand." The plan was to groom the young men and teach them the culture, the language, and the literature of the Babylonians. And it's interesting to note that Daniel cooperated during most of the training. There's no hint of anger or defiance; that is, until suppertime. When Daniel was assigned special food and drink that came directly from the king's table, his problems began.

Most of us would have welcomed the choicest fare and the finest wine. This time I picture Ina or even the Pioneer Woman. The problem was, Daniel was a good Jewish boy, and the food prepared for him wasn't kosher. It was considered "ceremonially unclean" because it had been offered up in pagan rituals.

So, instead of partaking, and even justifying his behavior by saying, "Well, this is the least I deserve," Daniel took a pass. He asked for permission not to "defile" himself by eating the food and drinking the wine.

Bottoms Up

It's hard for most of us to relate to the "ceremonially unclean" matters of the Old Testament. So, let's make it contemporary. Let's use alcohol as an example. It has a significant place in our culture, and the beverage industry is enormous. And, unlike food, alcohol isn't a survival tool. It just feels like it sometimes.

Personally, I don't drink alcohol, which, by the way, has cost me. I've been on the receiving end of a kind of reverse discrimination where people pass judgment and assume the worst. I'm either a recovering alcoholic or a religious fanatic. But I can assure you that neither is true. I simply don't like the taste of alcohol. In fact, every time I sip it, it reminds me of the time I used fingernail polish remover and then touched my lips before washing it off. *Yum. Bartender, hit me again.*

Also, I've never been wild about feeling out of control, which is probably a throwback to my panic disorder days. That was no picnic. And I've never needed alcohol to have fun either. I've discovered that a good time has more to do with the company I keep than the beverages I drink.

My husband, on the other hand, is a completely different story. He loves the taste of beer and was a good-time guzzling frat boy when we met in college. After we got married, though, he did something quite amazing. As we started our family, he decided to abstain completely . . . at least for a while. Looking back, it was an incredible sacrifice, and it must have taken an enormous amount of self-control.

He began to rethink the whole idea of having alcohol in the house when, one day, our little boy was standing by the refrigerator door. When I opened it, he grabbed a can of beer, brought it to my husband, and said, "Here's your pop, Daddy!" In that moment, my husband will tell you he had a bit of an epiphany. He decided to give up alcohol altogether until the kids were grown.

Now, obviously, this isn't everyone's conviction, nor does it need to be. Clearly, my husband had every right to drink an occasional beer. Alcohol is legal, within limits. It's even connected with the first miracle Jesus performed when he turned the water into wine at a wedding celebration in Cana (John 2). But my husband had seen the fallout of alcoholism and decided to put boundaries in place while our kids were young and impressionable. He understood the dangers of drinking and decided to do an incredibly unselfish thing. A Romans 14 kind of thing. He decided to forfeit his own right to do something purely for the wellbeing of someone else, lest he cause another to stumble, as the apostle Paul put it (v. 20).

Now, years later, the kids are grown, and let me tell you this: my hubby enjoys a cold one on a hot day. Also, I must admit, the verdict is still out for me on whether modeling complete abstinence is the way to go. Teaching moderation as a life skill is really important. But whenever I hear my husband crack open a cold beer after a hot round of golf, and he takes that first long swig and lets out an *Ahhh*, I'm reminded of the sacrifice he made. Hard as it is for me to understand, he actually enjoys the taste of beer, almost as much as I enjoy my hot coffee in the morning.

Obviously, as with so many self-control issues, the rules for drinking will be different for everyone depending on personal convictions, past issues, and/or family history that may put them at risk. And drunkenness is always frowned upon in Scripture simply because losing control puts people in danger of making bad choices. (Can I see a show of hands?) But forbidding alcohol altogether is not a biblical mandate, though some might wish it were.

Jill Briscoe used to tell the story of a preacher in England who was dead set against any type of alcohol consumption. When he came to the passage in 1 Timothy 5 where the apostle Paul instructs Timothy to take some wine to quiet his tummy troubles, the preacher insisted Paul didn't mean for Timothy to drink it. He claimed Paul was instructing Timothy to rub it on his stomach instead.

Alcohol, food, money, sex—it doesn't matter what our issues are, Daniel speaks to them all. And that's a good thing because it's hard to maintain any lasting sense of contentment when our behavior is out of control.

How It Works

Tucked neatly in the first chapter of Daniel is a great example of how self-control works. It says that the official who'd been placed in charge of training the prisoners was "sympathetic" to Daniel. He liked Daniel, but he was also nervous. He worried that if the king saw Daniel refusing the royal food and wine, and then looking worse than the other young men, his official head would roll. So, Daniel told the official to test him and give him nothing but vegetables to eat and water to drink for ten days. Then the official could judge for himself how Daniel looked. Sure enough, after ten days, Daniel looked better than the others. So, the official took away his choice food and wine and gave him water to drink and vegetables to eat instead. (Some reward.)

This bit of Scripture, which, by the way, is where the popular *"Daniel Diet"* comes from, is hardly rocket science. Vegetables and water are pretty sure bets when it comes to dieting. But we get desperate in our self-control battles, and we want something groundbreaking.

Someday I'm going to write a groundbreaking diet book. It will contain exactly four words. And it will guarantee success. *Eat less, exercise more.* Done. I'll set it next to my other bestseller on the topic of relationships. It too will guarantee success and contain only one word: *Kindness.*

It's Always Something

When we think about the vices Americans struggle with most, our thoughts tend to veer toward juicy storylines on reality TV. The ones filled with lots of champagne and adultery. But according to surveys conducted by the Barna Group, our struggles aren't quite that interesting. In fact, salacious sins are farther down the list than we might think.

According to the data, our top three self-control issues are: procrastination (60 percent), overeating (55 percent), and spending too much money (41 percent). Boring but true. Which is not to say that our less interesting sins are harmless, as anyone who struggles with them can attest.

In her book, *The Willpower Instinct*, health psychologist Kelly McGonigal defines willpower as "the ability to do what you really want to do when part of you really doesn't want to do it." Through her research at Stanford University, McGonigal identified the same pattern of temptations as the Barna Group. Food cravings and procrastination topped the list. Her findings also included some "attitude" issues, such as the urge to complain or be sarcastic.

But that's nothing. Most of us could fill a page with our self-control issues, I thought as I listened to a couple TED Talks on the *seven deadly sins*. According to the experts, America's top three self-control issues made the list.

The list of the seven deadly dandies goes way back and has evolved with time. In its current form, the list includes: (Quick! Can you name them?)

1. Sloth
2. Gluttony
3. Greed
4. Envy
5. Pride
6. Lust
7. Wrath

Aristotle wrote his best-known work about vices called *Nicomachean Ethics*. It was inspired by the works of another great philosopher, Plato, who was a friend and a teacher to a third great philosopher, Socrates. (This wraps up our history of philosophy lesson for today. You're welcome.)

All three philosophers explored the concept of human behavior. And though they go back several millennia, these issues hardly originated with them. Centuries earlier, King Solomon ruled Israel and famously wrestled to understand human nature. Solomon concluded that as long as humans are free to make their own choices, the struggle to make the right one will remain. Unless, of course, we change the rules of right and wrong.

According to some of the TED Talks I listened to, the seven vices could be slightly altered to present a more positive spin. Greed can become wealth, and wealthy people can help those in need. Envy can motivate us to work harder, and then we perform better, and so on.

But it was Christopher Ryan's handling of "lust" that fascinated me most. His dissertation was on the prehistoric roots of human sexuality. This became the basis for his book, *Sex at Dawn*, which carefully constructs the evolutionary argument that monogamy is "unreasonable" because it's "unnatural." According to Ryan, humans are among the few mammals that mate for life, which is why we struggle so much with temptation.[1]

His talk reminded me of an issue of *Time* magazine I saw

several years ago. The cover had a picture of a broken wedding band and a tagline that read, "Infidelity: It May Be in Our Genes." Like Ryan, author Robert Wright also argued that we might be "hardwired" for cheating. I agree that people should be free to make their own choices. But it occurs to me that like Ryan, Wright does a fantastic job of systematically removing one of our best motivators for willpower: God. Wright believes there is no God to be accountable to, which, by default, means there's no God to be empowered by. According to Wright, we're all just a random collection of DNA responding to our arbitrary surroundings.

I must admit that as I finished listening to Ryan's TED Talk, it left me feeling as though I'd just been handed a really good excuse for bad behavior. A free ticket for selfish indulgence.

Willpower is about putting into place everything you need to make the best choice.

Infidelity may sound highly evolved, but it comes with a steep price. I see evidence of this regularly as I speak to people across the country. It feels like betrayal any way you slice it. And the fallout is enormous because betrayal doesn't heal quickly.

When Wright's article was first published, I remember my pastor, Stuart Briscoe, having something to say about it. In his very proper English brogue, he reminded us, "Infidelity isn't about what's *in* our genes, it's about learning to keep our jeans *on*." It's that simple. Willpower is about putting into place everything you need to make the best choice. And don't fool yourself. At the end of the day, it is our choice, no matter where we are on our evolutionary journey.

A Clue to the Universe

Don't get too excited, but I think I may have discovered the clue to the universe. It's in Daniel chapter 1. Two little words that reveal *the* secret to contentment. Okay, maybe I'm not the first to discover it, but I'm just as excited.

In Daniel 1:8, we read that Daniel *resolved* not to defile himself. Then, in verse 9, it says, God *caused* the official to show him favor. Those two words, *resolved* and *caused*, are the picture of balance for a person of faith. They look very much like two other words found in Scripture that are also a clue to the universe . . . *plans* and *determines*. Proverbs 16:9 says, "We can make our *plans*, but the Lord *determines* our steps" (emphasis added).

These few words set up an incredible theological concept . . . the sovereignty of God. God's sovereignty, or His supreme control, is a mystery that both liberates and frustrates us. On a good day we celebrate it, but on a bad day it seems impossible to reconcile with a "good" God. The concept of God's sovereignty is such a mystery, it brings out the passion in some people. Churches have actually split trying to nail down how God can allow freedom but maintain control at the same time.

But how can we explain something only God can comprehend? And frankly, who would want a God they can fully comprehend? As the saying goes, "If God were small enough for us to comprehend, He would not be large enough for us to worship." But there is a balance we can all move toward, a place that can strengthen our faith and transform our contentment.

Our Part . . .

First, we need to do our part.

Every morning, before our feet touch the floor, we have a choice to make. We can either invite God into our day or we can go it alone. And let's not make this more complicated than it is. Sometimes I think we spend so much time worrying about whether God will do His part that we neglect simply to do ours.

If we want to be successful amid temptation the way Daniel was, if we want to *resolve* not to defile ourselves, we need to put a plan of action in place. A realistic and workable plan, such as seeing a doctor, getting counseling, or joining a support group. We might need to get rid of the movie channel, clear out the junk food, or remove the alcohol from our juice bar. When Daniel sensed trouble looming by the way things were moving, he came up with another plan. He reassured the nervous official by offering an alternative menu, a simple kosher meal.

We also see from the text that Daniel had friends who came alongside him. The Scripture says that among those who were handpicked from the prisoners of Judah were three other guys, Hananiah, Mishael, and Azariah. Or we may know them better by the names the chief official gave them: Shadrach, Meshach, and Abednego.

There is strength in numbers, and we need each other. We need people to be honest with us. Not to the point of destruction, but simply to broaden our perspective. "Plans fail for lack of counsel, but with many advisers they succeed" (Proverbs 15:22).

Figuring out who to let into our little worlds may take a little discernment. I love the story of the young man who approached a little old lady who was blind and waiting to cross a busy street. The man asked, "Can I cross with you?"

"Sure," the woman answered, reaching for his arm.

The two stepped off the curb, but their trip quickly turned treacherous. They zigged and zagged while angry drivers sped by honking and yelling obscenities.

Once safely to the other side, the woman became furious and demanded, "What's the matter with you? We were almost killed! Are you blind or something?"

The young man answered, "Yes. That's why I took your arm!"

This story reminds me of how important it is to know

who we're listening to or being influenced by. In Mathew 15:14, Jesus said, "If the blind leads the blind, both will fall into a pit."

Rolling Stone magazine had an article that talked about how difficult it is for rock stars to stay grounded. When everyone around them is starstruck, they're only told what they want to hear. Though you hardly need to be a rock star for that to happen.

Cleaning up after a dinner party one night, I commented to my husband how enjoyable the evening was. Then I realized why. Everyone seated at my table that evening held similar viewpoints on nearly every issue that came up. The conversation was filled with, "You're so right!" and "That's so true!" The evening was like a FOX News or MSNBC lovefest, which is fine once in a while. But as with everything else, too much of a good thing can be harmful. We need to see the other side of things and invite people into our lives whose opinions have proven trustworthy and balanced. Then

When everyone around us sees problems we don't, that's a huge red flag.

we need to brace ourselves a bit for what might come next. *Incoming!* We need to be ready to hear what they might say.

When everyone around us sees problems we don't, that's a huge red flag. I've never understood people who think they have an edge on some information the rest of us are clueless about. Truth is not esoteric or hidden for a select few. Like the sweet people who knock at my front door and offer me their literature. When they ask me if I'll look at their material, I say yes, if they'll look at mine. I try to reassure them that truth can withstand the bright lights of interrogation. It's what sets us free. But they decline every time.

We need to face the facts and embrace the truth; however uncomfortable it feels at first. Embracing the kind of contentment we are called to, specifically through the power of self-control, will require complete honesty and total resolve on our part. Then, when we do our part and plan our course, we can rest assured God will do His. He will determine our steps and show us where success and contentment are truly found.

God's Part . . .

When my kids were young, I decided to do an experiment to prove a point about our struggle with self-control. My experiments don't always work, but this one did . . . which, of course, is why I'm mentioning it.

We had a German shepherd named Ace. We got him as a puppy from a German breeder who strongly recommended obedience training. The trainer particularly wanted me to go through the classes since I'd be home most of the time with the dog and the kids. The breeder was kind but very firm. Old world Germany, for sure. When I took Ace to the first session, the breeder stood back for a few moments with his arms folded and simply watched the dynamics between puppy and me. Then, suddenly, he pointed his finger, and in a thick accent he said, "No, no, no! You talk way too much."

I was startled, and slightly offended. But I listened as he explained how too many words were confusing for the dog. Ace needed one-word commands. *Stay. Sit. Down. Front.* Like most well-trained Shepherds, Ace turned into a very disciplined dog. But like the rest of us, he had his weaknesses. His involved tennis balls and lunchmeat.

Ace routinely walked around with two tennis balls shoved in his mouth. He was pathetic and wanted so badly for us to play fetch with him. But whenever we agreed to play, and we told him to drop the balls, his internal conflict began. On the one hand, he wanted to let go of them simply for the joy of being able to pick them up again. But he couldn't bring himself to let go. The battle inside was brutal. We could see it in his face.

He is the reward and "rewarder of those who diligently seek Him."

The lunchmeat addiction Ace had was brutal too. He had sort of a sixth sense about it. No matter where he was in the house, somehow he always knew when someone was about to make a sandwich. The refrigerator door would open, and he would appear out of nowhere. One day, I decided to do a little experiment on self-control. I'd heard about similar ones, so I called my kids into the kitchen and said, "Watch this."

I grabbed a handful of lunchmeats, closed the refrigerator door, and there was Ace . . . undressing my fingers with his eyes. I said, "Sit" and he sat. Then I dropped the meat on the floor in front of him and moved across the kitchen.

I walked backward so we could keep our eyes locked, and it was amazing. Ace never took his eyes off me. He didn't steal a glance at the pile of lunchmeat sitting on the floor. He didn't even blink. But we knew what he was thinking. The drool that clung to his lips told us that.

Finally, at my one-word command, I said "Okay!" and Ace devoured the meat with one gulp. Then I turned to my kids and said, "This is how it has to be when you're facing temptations in life. Keep your eye on the Master. He is the reward and "rewarder of those who diligently seek Him" (Hebrews 11:6 NKJV).

Chapter Eleven

HOPE SPRINGS ANEW

III. Mind (renew our minds)

Sometimes I wonder if the apostle Paul mentions "the mind" last in Romans 12 for emphasis, sort of like an exclamation point. It's really the most important aspect of who we are, because if our head is in the wrong place, it's likely that the rest of us is too. Every behavior done in the body begins in the mind, that mysterious space between our ears where we process life, form opinions, and make our plans. It's what enables us to manage households, run businesses, and invent the next big thing.

Working with women has shown me how intuitive and creative we can be. When our mind's energy is harnessed, it can brainstorm groundbreaking solutions. But left to its own devices, it can steer us right off a cliff. We've all heard stories of intelligent people who've made bad decisions that cost them everything. It's like their red-flag radar was disconnected.

I listened as a young woman blissfully told me about the older man she was about to marry. He'd already been married and divorced several times, so I asked, "Why did the marriages fail?" Without missing a beat, she said, "They were the wrong women." *Red flag.*

Then there was the dad who asked whether he should keep lending his grown son money. He liked helping in a pinch, and what parent wouldn't? Then he added, "He likes to gamble, though, and that's a little disconcerting." *Red flag.*

Or the woman who told me she was involved with her daughter's married soccer coach. They really connected, she said, but it was harmless. They just needed someone to talk to. *Red flag.*

Learning how to make good decisions is essential. Understanding why we tend to make the decisions we do is the perfect place to start.

Soup or Salad?

The best way to ruin a good life is to make a bad decision. And some of us are really bad decision makers. Proverbs 3:13 (ESV) says, "Blessed is the one who finds wisdom." But where is this life-affirming wisdom found? It's not enough simply to listen to the "experts" anymore, because if the internet is any indication, everyone is an expert. And personality seems to have a lot to do with our decision-making process. Some people can make quick decisions. They close their eyes and jump and then sleep like a baby at night. But the rest of us struggle, then lie awake thinking about the thing that got away from us.

Discontentment can become the breeding ground for bad choices.

We expect to sweat, at least a little, over the monumental decisions, like who to marry or what business to merge. But what bugs us is when we stand in the rug department at Target grappling over which throw rug to buy. And the ability to make bad decisions doesn't seem to discriminate. It includes all races and genders.

Discontentment can become the breeding ground for bad choices. That's why financial planners instruct people to wait at least a year after the death of a spouse before making big decisions, such as selling a home or remarrying. But whenever we're about to make a significant decision, it's important to explore what's at our core. Are we trying to compensate for some unmet need? Is the choice we're making based on sound judgment or emotion? How will the decision impact those around us? And, perhaps the most revealing question of all: Would I tell my best friend to make the same choice?

In his blog called *Barking Up the Wrong Tree*, Eric Barker mentions some of the more amusing bad decisions Americans have made. He begins by looking at the tattoo industry. Evidently there are plenty of people who've regretted getting ink, because according to the American Society for Aesthetic Plastic Surgery, in 2017 alone Americans spent nearly $30 million on tattoo removal.

"Ashley forever!" *Not.*

Barker makes a good point about the decision-making process. In a world that's saturated with information, he says we don't need all the information in the world to make the right choice. We just need the right information.

The thing that sets me apart from a "deist" is the understanding that God has not left us to our own devices to find wisdom. He isn't amused by us struggling to interpret circumstances and read nature. As a theist, I believe God has initiated dialogue with His creation and has even invited us to come to Him where wisdom is found. Again, why wouldn't He?

I spent a lot of time listening to the complaints of atheists and agnostics while writing my book on doubt. It got intense, at times, particularly when I agreed with some of their objections. Those who dabble in the anti-theist mindset, such as comedian Bill Maher, think it rather "egocentric" to believe that even if there were a God, He would care about us individually.

But once again I ask, why not? At the end of the day, it's

Maher's opinion against mine. It's at least a fifty-fifty split. But until he can offer me a better solution, one that isn't buoyed by the millions of dollars that insulate him from the real world, I find tremendous power in prayer. And it's definitely the kind of power, peace, and wisdom that I know I'm ill-equipped to conjure up on my own. Believe me.

Some Practical Tips . . .

Information is trendy. Wisdom is not. And looking around our world, common sense doesn't appear to be nearly common enough. So, it's always refreshing to find insights that have stood the test of time, including these five steps. They're extremely helpful whenever we need to make a big decision:

1. **Define your path.** Ask yourself if your choice is in alignment with the core values you've developed. And does it fit into your long-term goals?

2. **Ask someone you trust for advice.** Finding a person who has a track record that's proven wise, reliable, and unbiased will make all the difference. And it's worth asking, where do they get their wisdom?

3. **Make an honest list of the pros and cons.** If you can anticipate an outcome, good or bad, you'll be much better prepared for it. Remember, difficulty doesn't mean failure.

4. Don't ignore warning signs and red flags. When your feelings become like that annoying kid in the pool I love talking about, who yells, "Look at me!" every ten seconds, you may need to take a look. Even if it's just to shut the kid up.

5. Never stop asking God for guidance. Life gets cluttered and makes us lose sight of God's amazing provision of wisdom. He says, "Call to me and I will answer you and tell you great and unsearchable things you do not know" (Jeremiah 33:3).

When we've carefully done these five things, then we're ready to take the last step with confidence.

Close your eyes and jump.

A Good Choice for the Right Reason

It's hard to understand why we settle for bad choices, what really motivates us to make a bonehead decision. For example, one day I was jogging near my home, and a car full of boys playing loud music came up behind me. As they passed, they tossed a can of Coke out the window and drenched my feet. At first, I was just startled. Then I felt offended. Then, as I thought about it more, I began to wonder if the liquid on my legs was, indeed, Coke. I reached down and touched the

Looking around our world, common sense doesn't appear to be nearly common enough.

mysterious fluid and quickly surmised it was not. *Yuck!* Setting a new land-speed record, I bolted home, stripped off my clothes, and scrubbed myself silly.

The next day, my son, who was in high school at the time, nonchalantly asked me if someone had thrown something at my feet while I was jogging the day before. I was surprised he knew about the prank, and when I told him they had, he simply nodded and said, "They'll be by here shortly."

Sure enough, before I even had a chance to question him about it, the doorbell rang, and there stood two boys who hardly looked old enough to have a driver's license. They introduced themselves and nervously explained that they'd come to apologize for the day before. I agreed what they'd done was stupid, then I quickly forgave them and thanked them for coming. But as I closed the door, I wondered if it was genuine contrition that had brought them to my front step or something else, like the fear of God someone had put into them. Namely, my son.

Eventually the details came to light. Evidently, my son, who was captain of the hockey team at the time, had heard through the high school grapevine about what had happened. And he wasn't pleased. So, he decided to approach the boys in the cafeteria during lunch and calmly voice his displeasure. He pointed out their disrespect for his mom and asked each one of them what they intended to do about it. Remarkably, all three of them agreed that an apology sounded like a really good idea.

Later, as I thought about what might have motivated the boys' stupidity, I thought about what motivates any of us to make bad decisions. Anger, boredom, fear, or something more? We make bad choices for lots of reasons, from sheer laziness to serious spiritual hunger. But the best way I know to avoid going over a cliff, whether in one fell swoop or one step at a time, is having priorities in the right place. That way, even when you're not paying attention, you're paying attention. This becomes a life skill according to King Solomon, who made his share of bonehead decisions too. (We'll talk about that later.) He wrote,

> Do not let wisdom and understanding
>   out of your sight,
>   preserve sound judgment and discretion;
>   they will be life for you,
>   an ornament to grace your neck.
>   (Proverbs 3:21-22)

Notice that Solomon doesn't say that things will always run smoothly with the right choice. Or that life will be easy. He says good choices will lead to life itself. He compares fullness and contentment to a beautiful piece of jewelry, like a necklace made of diamonds or gold.

Mysteries of the Mind

When neuroscientists talk amongst themselves, they talk about chemical synapses and neurotransmitters. When they're dumbing things down for the rest of us, they divide the mind into two parts. The *conscious mind* is where we think and make our decisions. It's where we decide, soup or salad. The *unconscious mind* is where we don't need to think. Most of us forget we have a digestive tract until it decides to remind us. It sounds simple enough, but even now, with all we've conquered in the scientific realm, the mind remains a mystery. For example, why do we wrestle with our thoughts? Do they control us, or do we control them? Philosophers, theologians, and psychologists have a field day with this type of question. And, ultimately, they all have something of value to contribute to the debate.

Sharon Begley is a science journalist for *The Wall Street Journal*. In her book, *Can't. Just. Stop.*, Begley looks at compulsive behavior and makes a distinction between an addiction and a compulsion. An addiction is a behavior that typically begins with a "joyous" outcome. It's something we want to repeat. A compulsion, on the other hand, has its roots in anxiety. It's a behavior we repeat to drain our anxious feelings.

Recently, while speaking at a women's conference on the empowerment of self-control, I shared my own experiences with compulsive behavior. Thirteen years of panic attacks taught me more about anxiety disorders than I ever wanted to learn. For years, I lived with a pulmonary system that was fueling adrenaline and anxiety into my system. I thought my anxious tendencies were a personal weakness and something I was bringing on myself. Then, one day, while walking through a Kmart in South Carolina, I found a little paperback called *Hope and Help for Your Nerves* by Dr. Claire Weekes. In the 1960s, Dr. Weekes was a game-changer in the field of anxiety disorders. Her insights into brain function helped me hang in there for thirteen years until I was finally diagnosed and treated.

In her book, Dr. Weekes explains how obsessions begin and how they can be relieved. She tells the story of a nurse who was struggling with some disturbing thoughts. The more she tried to put them out of her mind, the more trapped they became. The woman had been carrying a baby in her arms when she passed a window and suddenly thought, *What if I couldn't stop myself and threw this baby out the window?* She was so horrified at the vision, the thought began to haunt her, and she couldn't shake it.

Dr. Weekes offered a soothing solution. First, she pointed out to the woman the harmlessness of random thoughts. Disturbing or not, all people have fleeting thoughts that pop in and out of their heads all day long. The only difference was that the woman was making much more out of it than most people would. The doctor explained how fear and fatigue had made the woman highly sensitive. She'd been working late hours and in her vulnerable state, she completely overreacted, and it frightened her. The more exhausted she became by trying not to think about it, the more embedded the thoughts became. The doctor instructed the woman simply to let the thoughts come and go without giving them any more attention than they deserved. In time, through rest and diversion, the thoughts would simply lose their punch.

And they did.

Training Our Thoughts

Learning to take control of our thoughts is important because so many images compete for our attention. But short of brainwashing, such as the kind in the 1962 film *Manchurian Candidate*, we get to decide what we'll focus on. That's good, because the dangers are everywhere, even in "seemingly" safe places.

I have the evening news to thank for introducing my son to a brand-new term: oral sex. (Thank you, President Clinton.) Now, I realize he would have learned the term eventually anyway, but I can still see him standing in front of me and asking what it meant. There he was, all sweet and innocent, with those big blues eyes. Stalling for time, I decided to use the Socratic method

> *Learning to take control of our thoughts is important because so many images compete for our attention.*

and answered his question with another question. I asked him what *he* thought it meant.

"I think it means talking about sex," he said. *Good enough.*

As with most things, the internet is a two-edged sword. It's a fabulous source of information and connection, but its dangers make things tricky for parents trying to protect their kids. Unplugging can be a temporary solution, but the sooner we help young people develop the ability to monitor their own behavior, the better off they'll be. Any behavior that produces pleasure hormones can become addictive. And while the addict would like the high to last forever, the crash landing is inevitable. Addictions that thrive in secrecy are even more difficult to break because they're rarely conquered alone, which is complicated by the fact that they are "secret" sins.

Addictions often require help from a qualified counselor, a support group, or an accountability partner. (Preferably not a spouse. Too close.) They may necessitate a doctor's appointment and/or medication. And they will always require some kind of "replacement" therapy, which is why it's important to understand the unmet need that caused the addiction in the first place.

And training our brains can't begin too soon. When my son was about five, we were standing in the checkout line at the grocery store when he noticed the magazine rack filled with beautiful women. Their bulging bustlines weren't lost on his tender eyes as he pointed to the pictures and said a bit too loudly, "Mom, look at them."

All eyes turned our direction as I rushed him through the line and whispered something lame like, "That's not very nice."

A week later, we found ourselves in the same grocery store, in the same checkout line, faced with the same magazines with the same bulging cleavage. The only thing different was the faces. But this time, my son pointed to the covers and said, "Mom, they're gross, aren't they?" I stood there for a moment as his entire sexual future flashed before my eyes. I thought about the gay man I'd heard say, "My mom told me never to touch, and I never did."

Switching gears quickly to damage control, I said, "No, Matt. These women are not gross. They're beautiful. And they're bodies are beautiful. God made them beautiful." (The airbrush didn't hurt, but that was a discussion for another day.) "It's just that their bodies are special and private. We shouldn't be looking at them, and they shouldn't be showing us."

I watched my son's face as he processed this new information. *Appreciate the beauty, respect the body.* Now all grown up, he does both, which is as it should be. Though that appreciation does bring on a whole new set of self-control challenges.

It was King David who asked the million-dollar question, "How can a young man keep his way pure?" (Psalm 119:9 ESV). He'd succumbed to his own lust, with dire consequences, and he was able to answer his own question with insight he'd gained the hard way. It was pain that taught him to say, "I have stored up your word in my heart, that I might not sin against you" (v. 11 ESV).

A mind that's shaped by truth will thrive. But that's a deliberate act. Paul says in Romans 8:5, "Those who live according to the flesh have their minds set on what the flesh desires, but those who live in accordance with the Spirit have their minds set on what the Spirit desires."

The choice is ours, and that's a good thing. Because given the chance, we can get addicted to almost anything. And the pleasure hormones of any addiction make a habit hard to break.

Addiction Breaking

Breaking an addiction will require us to do a little soul-searching. We need to understand the empty spaces our bad habits are trying to fill. Otherwise, one harmful addiction will simply be replaced by another.

Tech researcher and blogger Justin Brown and his team at Ideapod study the ways in which media are produced and how they shape our thinking. In a 2017 post, Brown tackled the subject of porn. He titled the article, "Harvard Scientist Reveals the Shocking Impact of Watching Porn."

Obviously, people's opinions differ greatly on what constitutes pornographic material. What one labels offensive and degrading, another may call art or recreation. And, as with any addiction, the real mystery is why some people can take it or leave it, while others can develop a compulsion that overwhelms them. Either way, there seems to be plenty of research to sound an alarm, whether studies are conducted by people who oppose pornography on moral grounds or by those who defend it as free speech. I like to look at both sides of an argument to gather my information . . . you know, like back in the olden days, when the news media allowed us to form our own opinions.

Brown began his article by emphasizing the widespread availability of porn on the internet, and how easy it is to stream for free. Well, almost free. According to Harvard research, porn can be costly. And not just in the obvious ways, such as challenging intimacy in relationships. (Let's face it, who can compete with an airbrush?) Like all addictions, it can become insidious to our brains.

Kevin Majeres is a faculty member at Harvard Medical School, and a psychiatrist who specializes in cognitive behavioral therapy. He began his research on porn's effects by studying the mating patterns of rats. (Of course he did.) Majeres says:

> Scientists have discovered that if you place a male rat in a cage with a receptive female, they will mate; but once done, the male rat will not mate more times, even if the female is still receptive. He loses all sexual interest. But if, right after he finishes with the first female, you put in a second receptive female, he will immediately mate again; and again a third, and so on, until he nearly dies.[1]

Until he nearly dies? This could be hilarious if it weren't so serious. And according to Majeres, these findings line up with what researchers call the Coolidge effect, which has been found in every animal studied.

Majeres explains how dopamine, the brain's pleasure hormone, can cause addictive behavior. Dopamine screams, "Go for it! Do whatever it takes!" "When someone clicks and sees a new pornographic image, his lower brain thinks this is the real thing, . . . and so he gets an enormous dopamine flood in his upper brain, causing a wild amount of electrical energy." Majeres points out that this is a new phenomenon. This isn't something our ancestors were familiar with back when the pickins were slim.

But in our culture, where a dopamine binge is within our reach, "gaming the system," as Majeres puts it, becomes a vicious circle, which explains the nature of all addictions. When the brain is overstimulated by dopamine, some of the receptors are destroyed. And with fewer receptors available, it takes more to achieve the same dopamine thrill.

So, you may ask, if that happens, what is a person to do? Majeres explains that you need to stimulate other emotions to up the ante. For example, with porn use, it may involve kinkier behavior that elicits feelings of fear or disgust.

Yikes. And just think, all of this can be done in the privacy of one's own home. Long gone are the days when you actually had to walk into a store to purchase porn and risk being looked at as being depraved. *Price check for the pervert in aisle 5!*

These days, in a world that prides itself on open-mindedness and an "anything goes" mentality, the underbelly of the porn industry is painfully emerging. Internet child porn and its connection to human trafficking is a modern-day tragedy, and it begins with thoughts gone wild. Left to themselves, our thoughts can become obsessed with anything.

No one wants to forfeit personal freedoms or be told what to think. But long before Harvard brain studies were conducted and cutting-edge data were available, we were issued some sobering advice by the apostle Paul in 2 Corinthians 10:5: take each thought captive before it captures you.

Sin or Sickness

But what happens when we can't take our thoughts captive? When it's no longer a matter of willpower or decision? The line that separates mental illness from sinful behavior can be hard to define, which is why I'm glad God's the judge and I'm not. In fact, while struggling with depression, I got tired of hearing I should "be joyful." And when I was struggling with an anxiety disorder, I got tired of hearing I should "be anxious for nothing."

And sometimes the stakes get even higher. I was a young mom in 1994 when I witnessed the horror of another young mom named Susan Smith. I can still see the look of desperation on her face as she spoke to the news camera and pleaded for help. She'd been carjacked, she said, by a black man who kidnapped her children. Everyone was glued to their televisions as we watched the nation mobilize in the frantic search. Then the bomb dropped. In the days that followed the young mom's call for help, authorities were finding discrepancies in Smith's account. We watched as she became trapped in her own web of lies.

Smith finally admitted she'd made up the story. She'd murdered her own kids. She strapped them in their car seats and allowed her car to roll into a lake where they drowned. Then, as if that wasn't horrible enough, she revealed her motive. She'd wanted to begin a new life with her boyfriend who had told her he wasn't interested in a "ready-made" family. Smith was convicted of murder and sentenced to life in prison.

Sadly, life lost some of its innocence for me that day, as I joined the ranks of those who cynically say, "Nothing surprises me anymore." And though this story, as well as the story of Andrea Yates, is extreme, it does illustrate how the lines between evil and illness can become blurred. What kind of mother could violate the intensely primal moral code to protect her own children?

Studies done on inner-city poverty have consistently indicated a strong link between mental illness and homelessness. Mental health experts in Chicago recently pointed out that most of the people we tend to cross the street to avoid are in desperate need of anti-psychotic medication. Again, this may seem extreme, but at what point is bad behavior no longer a choice, but rather a serious cry for intervention? I hope I never have to be on the deciding jury when the stakes get this high.

We seem to have a history of struggling to find the balance between justice and mercy. We're either so focused on the rules that we forget about grace or we toss the rules out altogether and call it grace. Some of us are too sensitive and some of us are not sensitive enough. Back in college I was living in a sorority house and paying for meals I never ate. Literally, I was never home. One day, pressed for cash like every other college student, I had a thought. Since I was already paying hundreds of dollars for food I wasn't eating, maybe I could help myself to a head of lettuce and a box of Saltines and take them with me.

So, before class the next morning, I went down to the kitchen with my backpack in tow. I grabbed a head of lettuce from the fridge and crackers from the shelf. And wouldn't you know it, the moment I shoved the food into my backpack, a sister walked in. We said hello as I walked out of the kitchen. I wasn't sure if she saw me take the food, but I felt ridiculously guilty. But the question is, was I guilty? I was paying for the meal plan, but it wasn't really a take-out service.

Guilt is an interesting concept, because we should feel guilty when we break rules. That bad feeling is a sign that our consciences are not too far gone. On the other hand, some of us struggle with too much remorse. The Greek word for conscience is *suneidesis*, which means "moral awareness." But I've often wondered about those of us whose *suneidesis-ness* is far too tender. Too much or too little, either extreme can be dangerous. And then, just to keep things interesting, there are times when "breaking the rules" seems permissible. In the Old Testament Book of Joshua, we read about a woman named Rahab who was a prostitute living in Jericho. According to the narrative, Rahab hid two spies whose lives were in danger and then she lied about it to protect them.

Centuries later, in the Book of Hebrews, Rahab was commended for her faith. She chose to obey a higher law, namely God's law rather than man's. But before we get all carried away with "bending the rules," we need to understand something about guilt. It was never designed to paralyze us. It was meant to keep our creative selves on track. That's how He sets the captive free.

Give Yourself a Break

And let's face it, on some level, we all need to be set free. Even King David, the man after God's own heart, needed to be set free from himself. I mean, what can you say about a "biblical hero" whose claim to fame is adultery and murder? In some ways David's failures should bring us comfort. It's good to know that such things can be forgiven. But in other ways, it should probably make us nervous, because if God's man, the second king of Israel, wasn't immune to epic failure, why should we think we are?

In 2 Samuel 11, when the king should have been occupied with more productive endeavors, such as leading his army in battle, he was at home and in bed. One night, unable to sleep, he strolled along the rooftop of the palace and spotted a lovely woman bathing. No one could fault David for the admiration he had for her beauty or for the thoughts that popped into his head. It's what he did with those images that became the problem. Not only did he send for Bathsheba and commit adultery with her, but when she wound up pregnant, he attempted to cover his tracks by having her husband Uriah, David's own soldier, killed on the front line.

David's fall is epic, but what's really staggering was his inability to acknowledge and deal with his sin. He was a follower of God and a leader of men! Yet so efficiently had he rationalized and compartmentalized his behavior, that by the time the prophet Nathan confronted him, he was in complete denial. *What problem?*

At first glance it would seem David had a conscience that was calloused to conviction. He seemed unaware of the depth of his transgression, seamlessly rationalizing his behavior. But good and evil cannot comfortably coexist in the life of a believer. David, who committed some serious sins—the big guys: adultery and murder—grew increasingly uncomfortable . . . and that's a good thing. The problem is when we don't see the problem and we overlook its painful warning signs.

Before he confessed his sin, David's oppression increased: "When I kept silent, my bones wasted away through my groaning all day long. For day and night your hand was heavy upon me; my strength was sapped as in the heat of summer" (Psalm 32:3-4). David's guilt was so intense, it crept into his body. His days were joyless, and his nights were sleepless. It was that nagging, oppressive feeling we get that's hard to shake, and we know something is just not right.

I've come to see that feeling of oppression as a warning sign. Though I've also come to realize that for people like me, a little "too" sensitive, those feelings aren't always accurate. But it is always worth a look.

Chapter Twelve

FINDING
THE PURPOSE

We've all heard that too much of a good thing can be dangerous. But too much contentment? Well, maybe. We've been designed to enjoy life and embrace it fully. People of all ages, cultures, and creeds know what it is to smile. But one of the dangers of things running too smoothly is that, too often, apathy can slip in quietly (a plague I'd like to suffer from a little more often than I do).

Rarely do we fall into bed at night having had the best day everr, and ask, "Where are you, God?" This is the kind of question reserved more for a day filled with stress and turmoil. We're meant to find joy on the journey, to explore, expand, and evolve. But we're also designed to connect with our Creator, and sometimes we need reminders.

It's like the little boy who's so busy running and playing

that his mom needs to grab him as he flies through the kitchen. "Come here, you," she says, as she squeezes him and plants a kiss on his head. The boy squirms a little in protest but not because he doesn't love his mom. He's just got cousins to chase.

Scripture is filled with examples of people who've ignored God. We read their accounts, and some of them are epic failures. Personally, I find their stories refreshing, and not because I like to see people struggle or because misery loves company. It's just that their honest accounts lend enormous credibility to the historicity of the Bible. I mean, who would ever create a religious book filled with so many losers? There are two other kings, besides David, who were written about in the Old Testament, and both fit the "epic failure" description. We hear about them occasionally, but each had a huge impact on my faith as a young speaker. The first one is Solomon, the third king of Israel, who reigned around 1000 BC.

We've been designed to enjoy life and embrace it fully.

Solomon amassed incredible wealth. He built the first temple in ancient Jerusalem, which stood until Nebuchadnezzar II brought it down six hundred years later. But what really sets him apart for me is his epic struggle with discontentment. I mean, the guy had everything. But, even so, Solomon struggled with an empty heart.

Pascal talked about this in the seventeenth century. The

mathematician-turned-philosopher identified an emptiness that's inside all of us. We can stuff that empty space with lots of different things, even good things and creative things. But, in the end, it's a God-shaped hole that only God can fill. This imagery always makes me think of that shape-sorting toy kids play with. Sometimes the pieces fit, and the game goes smoothly. Other times, nothing fits, and the toy gets kicked across the room. (I still have trouble matching my pots and pans to their lids.)

It's easy for a self-sufficient culture like ours to lose sight of our need for God. But I think rough patches in life can be celestial squeezes. And I think it's always been that way. Solomon admitted to having been given lots of celestial squeezes, but he was too busy racing through the kitchen to notice. He was distracted with more important things, like amassing wealth and chasing women.

I've always appreciated Solomon's honesty. Though one wonders how honest he would have been had he known we'd be discussing his journals today. He penned some of the most painful words in all of literature: "Vanity of vanities! All is vanity" (Ecclesiastes 1:2 ESV). Or in contemporary speak, "Meaningless, meaningless, life is meaningless."

I thought about how Solomon's words had a painfully familiar ring to them. They sounded a lot like Anthony Bourdain's words. The popular American chef tragically took his own life in June 2018. He, too, appeared to have everything. He was an author and a world traveler whose

TV show *Parts Unknown* attracted millions. Yet he, too, spoke candidly about his emptiness.

Rose McGowan is a former model and actress who is now an activist taking a stand against sexism in Hollywood. In an interview she had with Bourdain's girlfriend, Asia Argento, Argento said Bourdain struggled intermittently with deep depression. Unfortunately, he lived his life on the edge and only "sort of" listened to his doctor.

Last year, in an interview with *The Guardian*, Bourdain talked about some of his more regrettable choices, like his history of drug addiction and hurting so many people. He also described himself as an "unhappy soul." Bourdain was also a self-professed atheist, not that all atheists are unhappy. But he said he was often suspicious of religious people, which is understandable, especially if that's been your experience. I had *good* experiences, and I sometimes get suspicious of religious people, specifically the ones who mess up the message of God's grace.

As Bourdain traveled the planet and enjoyed things most of us can only imagine, I wonder how far he looked beyond the people, places, and things that can let us down. I wonder if he struggled to break free from the Arms that tried to grab him as he raced through the kitchen. I'd like to think he's not struggling to break free anymore. I'd like to think his empty cup is finally full, and it began with a kiss planted on his forehead.

I admire both Solomon's honesty and Bourdain's. I really

do. Some people "say" they admire honesty, then use your words against you. I've heard business leaders talk about the dangers of being too candid with colleagues. Often, a problem that's long since been resolved keeps resurfacing. Personally, I'm not much of a grudge holder or a scorekeeper. I have way too many skeletons in my own closet for that. I admire the fact that Solomon was honest and unafraid to ask the tough questions. I like tough questions. I wrote an entire book encouraging Christians to ask more tough questions.

Those questions led me to a sturdier, more refined faith. In fact, I've asked so many questions, I often challenge people to give me one I haven't thought of. Not that I have all the answers, mind you. It's just that I now know where to begin my search.

What's It All About?

In the Book of Ecclesiastes, Solomon wonders about the meaning of life, its purpose, and whether it has any lasting value. He questions the things so many of us pursue and then wonders why we pursue them. We toil to get rich, he says, then we simply die, and it goes to someone else. Pointless.

To compensate for the gaping hole inside him, Solomon poured himself into anything that might bring him relief: riches, knowledge, physical pleasure. He said, "I denied myself nothing my eyes desired; I refused my heart no pleasure" (Ecclesiastes 2:10). Yet, somehow, it wasn't enough.

Solomon said, "When I surveyed all that my hands had done and what I had toiled to achieve, everything was meaningless, a chasing after the wind; nothing was gained under the sun" (Ecclesiastes 2:11).

In Rick Warren's wildly popular book, *The Purpose Driven Life*, Warren begins with a very sobering statement that speaks to Solomon's dilemma. "The purpose of your life is far greater than your own personal fulfillment, your peace of mind, or even your happiness. It's far greater than your family, your career, or even your wildest dreams and ambitions. If you want to know why you were placed on this planet, you must begin with God. You were born *by* his purpose and *for* his purpose."[1]

> *When we're self-absorbed, we run the risk of feeling empty. It's like our hearts run dry and begin to scramble to find water.*

Warren was borrowing words from the apostle Paul, who wrote, "All things have been created through him and for him. He is before all things, and in him all things hold together" (Colossians 1:16-17). I think what Paul was referring to here was what he called the secret to contentment. While in prison he wrote, "I know what it is to be in need, and I know what it is to have plenty. I have learned the secret of being content in any and every situation, whether well fed or hungry, whether living in plenty or in want" (Philippians 4:12).

It wasn't power or possessions that set Paul or Solomon

free. It was the knowledge that God will make all things beautiful "in its time," as Solomon put it in Ecclesiastes 3:11, and that along the way, God will supply all our needs in Christ Jesus, as Paul put it in Philippians 4:19. And I can't help but notice that whenever Solomon took his focus off himself and placed it firmly on God, he started to enjoy things again. It's as though it gave him permission to declare all things—eating, drinking, and working—to be gifts from God to be savored and enjoyed.

When we're self-absorbed, we run the risk of feeling empty. It's like our hearts run dry and begin to scramble to find water. Like Solomon, we can fill the emptiness with lots of things, even good things. But at the end of the day, we'll thirst again. That's why Jesus offered the woman at the well something more. He saw into her heart and knew her struggle. Her search for contentment included men— five husbands, to be exact. So Jesus, totally sympathetic to her struggle, offered her something more. He offered "living water" from a well that never runs dry (John 4:10-14).

Another King

Then there's King Nebuchadnezzar, who reigned five hundred years after Solomon. His story reminds us that no matter how much we evolve as people, the human heart remains strangely the same. As Solomon put it, "There is nothing new under the sun" (Ecclesiastes 1:9).

In Daniel chapter 4, we read an account of Nebuchadnezzar standing at his palace, surveying the splendor of his kingdom. He said, "Is not this the great Babylon I have built as the royal residence, by my mighty power and for the glory of my majesty?" (Daniel 4:30). Talk about self-absorption. Most of us, when talking about our own kingdoms, would never say it quite that way—"my power, my glory"—but we may come close.

Nebuchadnezzar's story reminds me of the farmer who purchased an overgrown plot of land. He worked hard to cultivate it and make it productive. Every Sunday, the preacher would drive by the field on his way to church and see the man working. One morning, the preacher stopped and invited the farmer to church. And, as preachers are apt to do, he began praising God for the lush green fields that now surrounded the farmer.

The preacher said, "Friend, you've been blessed with a beautiful portion of God's green earth."

"Yes," the farmer replied, "but you should have seen how He kept it before I took over."

King Nebuchadnezzar worked hard and had everything he possibly could have wanted, except for one thing. Like Solomon before him, contentment eluded him. In Daniel 4, we see a deeply troubled man whose troubles were about to become even deeper. It all began with a disturbing dream that was filled with terrifying images. Most dreams are hardly worth mentioning, if we remember them at all, but this was the kind that sticks with you.

In Daniel 4, we read, "I, Nebuchadnezzar, was at home in my palace, contented and prosperous. I had a dream that made me afraid. As I was lying in bed, the images and visions that passed through my mind terrified me" (vv. 4-5). The terror of the images was so deep that Nebuchadnezzar became desperate for relief. So, he called in the kingdom's best: the magicians, the enchanters, the astrologers, the diviners. But no one could interpret his dream. Finally, a solution was found when Daniel was called in. He was a prophet by now, and as with all prophets, God used him as a mouthpiece.

Daniel listened to the king's dream, and you know how most dreams lose their punch when you try to describe them to someone? Well, this was not the case. In fact, even Daniel was struck by the graphic details. Nebuchadnezzar dreamt of a beautiful tree. It was large and Zen-like, with animals resting in its shade. Then a heavenly voice said, "Cut it down," and all that remained were the roots and a stump. The king knew the dream meant trouble. He only hoped it meant trouble for his enemies. But Daniel said, "My lord, if only the dream applied to your enemies and its meaning to your adversaries! The tree you saw, which grew large and strong, with its top touching the sky, visible to the whole earth, with beautiful leaves and abundant fruit, providing food for all, giving shelter to the wild animals, and having nesting places in its branches for the birds—Your Majesty, you are that tree!" (Daniel 4:19-22).

This was hardly the news Nebuchadnezzar was looking for. But, to the king's credit, his next words were not, "Off with his head!" Instead, the king allowed Daniel to speak and listened while the prophet announced the decree God had issued against him: "You will be driven away from people and will live with the wild animals; you will eat grass like the ox and be drenched with the dew of heaven. Seven times will pass by for you until you acknowledge that the Most High is sovereign over all kingdoms on earth and gives them to anyone he wishes" (Daniel 4:25).

Heading for a Breakdown

Clearly God was judging the king's sin. And what was the king's sin, you may ask? Nebuchadnezzar was guilty of being his own god. He was obviously a shrewd leader and a very effective businessman. All good. God has designed us to flourish. Jesus talks about the abundant life. But as Nebuchadnezzar succeeded, so too did his ego, and it was pushing him into God's territory where we have never been invited. God tried to get Nebuchadnezzar's attention. He gave him fair warning and plenty of time to change his ways. In fact, twelve months went by before God acted on his threat.

Then it happened. It was probably a day like any other, as Nebuchadnezzar walked along his rooftop. Maybe it was that lovely time of day that photographers call the golden hour, right after sunrise or right before sunset, when the light becomes soft. As Nebuchadnezzar surveyed his kingdom and again sang his own praises, it was obvious that he had no intention of repenting. Daniel tells us that the words were still on the king's lips when judgment came, and Nebuchadnezzar's world was rocked. He was struck down with some sort of an affliction, an emotional or a mental breakdown. He became disabled and no longer fit to run his kingdom, so his throne was taken from him.

Nebuchadnezzar became an outcast, forced to live in the fields with the animals. He became the picture of a disturbed, unkempt man—the kind you avoid. His hair grew like feathers and his nails like claws. It wasn't pretty.

Nebuchadnezzar had heard Daniel's words twelve months earlier. He'd listened. He may have even been moved by them. But life has a way of distracting us, and we forget. We all know what it's like to hear great lessons of faith on a Sunday morning only to forget them by Tuesday.

This is what James was talking about when he wrote:

Anyone who listens to the word but does not do what it says is like someone who looks at his face in a mirror and, after looking at himself, goes away and immediately forgets what he looks like. But whoever looks intently into the perfect law that gives freedom and continues in it—not forgetting what they have heard but doing it—they will be blessed in what they do. (James 1:23-25)

Nebuchadnezzar had looked in the mirror, but when he turned away, he forgot what he saw, and his struggle began. We're not exactly sure how long his affliction lasted. Daniel uses the phrase "seven times" to describe how long it would be before the king saw the error of his ways. But somehow, amid his confusion, Nebuchadnezzar had a moment of clarity. He paused, looked heavenward, and everything changed.

> At the end of that time, I, Nebuchadnezzar, raised my eyes toward heaven and my sanity was restored. Then I praised the Most High; I honored and glorified him who lives forever. His dominion is an eternal dominion; his kingdom endures from generation to generation. All the peoples of the earth are regarded as nothing. He does as he pleases with the powers of heaven and the peoples of the earth. No one can hold back his hand or say to him: "What have you done?" (Daniel 4:34-35)

I have circled in my Bible the words, "my sanity was restored." And I've highlighted, "Now I, Nebuchadnezzar, praise and exalt and glorify the King of heaven, because everything he does is right and all his ways are just. And those who walk in pride he is able to humble" (Daniel 4:37). These are important words. They remind me of something I tend to forget. God is in charge, and He has our back. And those who walk in pride, He is able to humble.

I know it's true, so why do I keep forgetting?

A Constant Battle

After my uncomfortable banquet experience in Milwaukee, you would have thought I'd learned enough lessons to last me a lifetime. But obviously, I needed a reminder.

I was asked to give a seminar at a women's conference at a large resort outside of Milwaukee. It had at one time been the Playboy Club, and if you looked closely, you could still see a purple tassel here and there. Good thing the walls couldn't talk.

On the day of the event, hundreds of us filed in. I was led to the speaker's table, and because I was still new to the speaking circuit, I remember feeling a little like royalty as I greeted the other speakers. As we listened to the opening announcements, I pulled from my folder instructions for the day and the list of seminars offered. I studied the site map to determine where my seminar would be. But when I matched the room number with my name, I figured there had to be a mistake. The room I was assigned to looked to be no bigger than a broom closet. And I know broom closets. They can hold three women or maybe four, if we scrunched in.

Didn't the coordinators think I could bring in a few more women than that?

The hiss was almost audible as the wind left my sails, and I was instantly convicted. Who did I think I was anyway? I glanced around the table, relieved no one could read my thoughts. I knew there were probably dozens of women attending the conference that day who could have done a better job than me. Just being included should have been enough. Silently I asked God to forgive me for my misguided pride. I told Him I was grateful just to be included that day. If three or four women were all that could squeeze into the broom closet, I prayed three or four women would leave feeling glad they came.

My emotions may have said one thing, but my mind said another.

When the emcee finally dismissed us, I picked up my notes and headed for the room where I was to give my seminar three times. The first talk went well. By the second one, it was standing room only. By the third, I was informed I'd be moved to the ballroom.

I got to the ballroom a little early and placed my notes on the podium. Looking out over the rows of empty chairs, I braced myself for another hit. *Lord, I'd rather speak to a crowded broom closet than to an empty ballroom.* But this time I was ready. My emotions may have said one thing, but my mind said another. God was in charge, not me, and the women who lined the crowded hallways that day were His, not mine.

Liberated once again by God's sovereignty, I stood back and watched as one by one the women filed into the ballroom. Soon every chair in the place was taken.

This must be what the apostle Peter meant when he wrote, "Humble yourselves, therefore, under God's mighty hand, that He may lift you up in due time" (1 Peter 5:6). In due time. In His time. In His way.

Chapter Thirteen

TOOLBOX

I was sitting with my friend on her back deck when a bird flew into one of her freshly washed windows. He swooped in at full tilt, and the thud was disturbing. As he lay motionless, we pretty much knew he was dead. It was hard to watch. Then, after a few moments, he began to show signs of life, which was even harder to watch because he really struggled. I was reminded of how much I hate to see suffering. I know he was just a bird, but, come on, I was brought up on Walt Disney. I knew there had to be a mama bird somewhere setting the table for dinner, looking at the clock, and getting worried.

If I had my choice, no one would struggle, not even a bird. We'd all be happy all the time. But we do struggle. And though I'm not completely sure why, it's obvious that God had no intension of creating a race of robots that couldn't feel things, make choices, or live with consequences. We've also been wired to display a great deal of empathy. We feel better when we alleviate someone's pain . . . unless there's something seriously wrong with us.

This makes discipline tricky. The hardest part of parenting is figuring out how much we should push our kids and how much we should help them. This was illustrated perfectly on an episode of *Modern Family* when the crazy Cameron and Mitchell were trying to "Ferberize" their daughter, Lilly.

The hardest part of parenting is figuring out how much we should push our kids and how much we should help them.

Dr. Ferber invented a method that's supposed to teach children to sleep through the night. It involves letting them cry without rescuing them too quickly, so they can learn how to "self-soothe." The jury is still out on the merits of Ferberizing. And it's hard to know who suffers more, the parent or the child. But Mitchell was furious with Cameron because he kept sneaking into Lilly's room to comfort her. According to Mitchell, Cameron was denying her the opportunity to learn how to comfort herself, an important life skill. Cameron, on the other hand, was unable to bear the sound of Lilly's crying and even questioned Mitchell's ability to feel compassion. I think the term "heartless monster" came up.

I totally felt for Cam on this one. Ignoring a child's cry seems unnatural. I can also see what Ferber was trying to get at. It's sort of the same argument used against a welfare system that's out of control. "Don't just give them a fish. Teach them how to fish."

As my friend and I stood on her deck watching the bird struggle, we discussed our options. Should we pick him up? Should we move him? I believe "mercy killing" even entered the conversation, though neither of us could've gone through with that. Then, just as I was planning the Scripture reading for his funeral, the bird started to move his wings. His tenacity was amazing. Flapping, then resting. Flapping, then resting. Within an hour, he had completely recovered. If he hurried, he'd still make it home in time for dinner.

As the bird flew away, I commented to my friend that it was a good thing we hadn't gone all Kevorkian on him. Which began another discussion on the moral implications of letting people suffer or putting them out of their misery. We agreed that there are times when suffering produces something valuable. Something that can't be obtained any other way. The Book of James talks about that. For me, there's also a strange dichotomy when it comes to suffering. While I have very little tolerance for watching others suffer, I've discovered I can endure quite a bit of discomfort myself. Especially if there's a point to it, such as with childbirth.

I've been strapping on my running shoes every day for twenty-five years, even when it hurts. I force myself to run several miles because I know there's a payoff. I know I'll be able to step onto the scale in the doctor's office without cringing. Otherwise, it can be brutal.

I realize that jogging, crying babies, and kamikaze backyard birds hardly hold a candle to the kind of suffering some people endure. But maybe there are lessons to be learned from all three. Think about it. Maybe, as James suggests, there are other ways of looking at our struggles. Maybe it just takes a bird's-eye view: "Consider it pure joy, my brothers and sisters, whenever you face trials of many kinds, because you know that the testing of your faith produces perseverance. Let perseverance finish its work so that you may be mature and complete, not lacking anything" (James 1:2-4).

Survival Skills

There are far more solutions to our discontentment than our painful emotions allow us to see. And, in the end, it isn't so much about what we have that matters but what we do with it that counts. It's no secret that channeling our pain into something useful is incredibly healing. Studies continue to bear this out. In fact, two of the most powerful weapons we can use to overcome our unhappiness are generosity and gratitude. Though I realize that nothing, and I mean NOTHING, appeals to us less when we're hurting.

In the thick of my depression, nothing sounded worse than being around other people. They annoyed me almost as much as I annoyed myself. But I knew the research was strong. Whenever we look outside ourselves and invest in somebody else's life, our lives get better.

Another study done by the University of Michigan continues to bear this out. According to an article published in the *Journal of Clinical Psychology*, the study examined two ways adults struggling with anxiety and/or depression try to increase their own sense of self-worth. One looked inward and the other looked out.

Dr. Seth J. Gillihan said that self-image (inward) goals "focus on 'obtaining status or approval and avoiding vulnerability during social interactions.' " The outward goals, however, were about "striving to help others and . . . making a positive difference in someone else's life."

Gillihan adds that this is mixed news for these adults. It's bad news for the inward crowd since this method often backfires. "It leaves us feeling depressed and anxious and damages our relationships. These two effects can reinforce each other, leading to a downward spiral." It's really good news for the outward crowd, however. "By turning our attention toward helping others, we make everyone feel better—ourselves included. We find not only relief from our depression and anxiety, but also improvements in our relationships."[1]

There are far more solutions to our discontentment than our painful emotions allow us to see.

Generosity

One gloomy day, while feeling particularly disgusted with myself, I decided to test the generosity theory. I knew it would require all my strength, but here is the thing about charity work, support groups, and other agencies we'd rather avoid: they are run by people who appreciate us just showing up.

I had clicked onto our church website to see the list of service opportunities, and though nothing sounded worse, I decided to take the first step . . . be it ever so slight. So, still in my sweats, I mustered the energy to brush my teeth, throw on a pair of sunglasses, and grab the car keys. I crept in the back door of the church and began stocking the shelves of the food pantry. They made it easy. I didn't have to think, speak, or look at anyone. *Dry goods on the left. Perishables on the right.*

As I drove home that day, I realized it wasn't nearly as bad as I had imagined. I could probably even do it again next week. So I did. And little by little, the tiny steps I took became a giant leap forward, just as the University of Michigan study had said. I was becoming another healthy statistic because in the process of helping others, I helped myself. I became living proof of the emotional survival skill called generosity.

And here's another thing about generosity. Letting others help us not only blesses us, but it genuinely blesses them too. Being too proud to receive a helping hand is almost as "self-absorbed" as withholding a helping hand from someone else. I learned that years ago.

When I was about eleven years old, we had a house fire. I remember it as if it was yesterday, and I'm reminded of it every spring when the world begins to bloom. Every April, when winter finally gives it up, the world comes back to life, and the thick scent of lilacs casts a spell over people like me who grew up in the Midwest. We become ten again. Sometimes the scent brings me back to the sixth grade, to the evening of my older brother's pre-prom party. My dad had just finished renovating our basement with fresh pine walls and new carpet. It was the perfect place to have a party.

As the kid sister, on the night of the dance, I could hang around just long enough to see the couples arrive. They looked like royalty to me, the girls in their long dresses and each boy in a tux. The basement came alive with laughter and music as my parents made appetizers upstairs.

After the party, the couples headed out, and my parents began the cleanup. I nibbled on the plates of leftovers that were still yummy as my folks went to work on the dishes in the sink. I can still see my dad standing in the kitchen with a dishtowel in one hand and a plate in the other.

He looked up and noticed a thick black cloud spreading quickly across the kitchen ceiling. It seemed alive as it slithered quietly. His eyes traced its source back to the basement door. And doing what we've all been instructed *not* to do, he opened the door, then quickly slammed it shut again when a huge billow of smoke filled the hallway. He yelled, "Get out of the house, everyone! There's a fire!"

My dad's words pierced through me like a bullet. And as I shoved our collie out the side door, it all felt a bit surreal. The evening air was sweet and still, a complete contrast to what was brewing inside. I could hear my mom dialing the operator, asking for the fire department, and momentarily forgetting our address. When she finally got it right, I circled around to the front porch and yelled through the screen to my older sister who was upstairs drying her hair. Standing in her robe, at the top of the stairs, she didn't take me seriously until she heard the commotion coming from the kitchen.

I remember standing quietly on the freshly mowed lawn with my dog sitting obediently by my side. Then, suddenly, the silence was broken by the faint sound of sirens coming from every direction. They grew louder by the minute, and soon our street was lined with emergency vehicles and crowds of people who seemed to have appeared from nowhere.

Gratitude can rescue us from discontentment too. But like generosity, it may be an acquired taste.

Some came by foot, still in their pajamas, others came by car or rode bikes. This was quite the attraction for our little town on an otherwise peaceful Saturday night.

On their way to the prom, my brother and his friends

decided to stop by the 7-Eleven. As they pulled into the parking lot, a car pulled up beside them. A kid looked over at my brother and said, "Hey, Kilroy, your house is on fire."

Eventually the fire was put out. We were told it was caused by a low burning candle that had been placed on a bookcase in the basement. The candle had been blown out but not before kindling the dry pine above it. Even today I find myself at parties warning the hosts about burning candles in enclosed spaces.

Once ignited, the secret flames quickly climbed up the heating duct that led to my sister's bed, where she would've been sleeping an hour later. This became one of those "what ifs" that kept my parents awake at night. It was a scary event, and the damage to our house was extensive. My dad's beautiful new basement was destroyed, and we were left homeless for quite a few months. But as with any kid, the seriousness of the situation was lost on me. All I knew was that we were forced to live in a hotel, and I finally got the swimming pool I'd been asking for. My sixth-grade popularity rating soared.

That warm spring evening, years ago, taught me something about the paradoxes of life. In those moments of intensity and fear, I saw friends and strangers gather around us and offer their homes and beds.

It was the kind of thing we hear about every night on the evening news, if we're listening. Mixed in the stories of trouble and despair are subplots of kindness and bravery. We see people selflessly rising and giving of themselves. Their generosity proves that life's worst situations can provide opportunities for our best to shine.

Gratitude

Gratitude can rescue us from discontentment too. But like generosity, it may be an acquired taste. It may be something we need to cultivate. It certainly didn't come naturally to me during my depression, so I knew I'd have to make an effort. I'd have to search for things to be grateful for. I knew they had to be there, somewhere.

At first, I found little things to be grateful for, mainly because my tender brain couldn't accommodate anything larger. My new mantra became, "This is a good moment."

Sitting on my parents' deck and smelling the cedar . . .

This is a good moment.

Lying in bed and knowing my kids are safely tucked in . . .

This is a good moment.

Soaking in a hot tub listening to Debussy . . .

This is a good moment.

I repeated this mantra over and over until, eventually, gratitude became second nature once again.

When the apostle Paul was imprisoned and facing possible execution, he wrote a letter to the church in Philippi. It was the kind of letter that most of us would be hard-pressed to write even on a good day and includes words that continue to stir the hearts of people around the world. They are words stitched on throw pillows and written in calligraphy on kitchen magnets and framed art. But when nothing feels right in our world, the words can fall flat. Sometimes they even annoy us. "Rejoice in the Lord always. I will say it again: Rejoice!" (Philippians 4:4). *Really?*

"Let your gentleness be evident to all," Paul says, "The Lord is near. Do not be anxious about anything, but in every situation, by prayer and petition, with thanksgiving, present your requests to God. And the peace of God, which transcends all understanding, will guard your hearts and your minds in Christ Jesus" (Philippians 4:4-7). This description of peace, or "not being anxious," as Paul puts it, seems like a tall order for people struggling with depression or anxiety. It was a very tall order for me in the thick of my panic disorder. Strangely, I found Paul's words to be both a comfort and a frustration, simultaneously. At times, I felt so battered inside, it was impossible to feel content. But I could taste it.

Encouragement

It's easy for our minds to fall victim to discouragement, which is why I'm so fascinated by people who overcome obstacles. Two of my favorite movies, both directed by Ron Howard, tell powerful true stories of tenacity and what it means to press through the pain. *A Beautiful Mind* is the story of John Nash, who won the Nobel Prize for Economics while suffering from schizophrenia. The other one is *Apollo 13*, which I watched again recently and was reminded of why it remains on my top ten list.

The real *Apollo 13* was launched on April 11, 1970, from the Kennedy Space Center. It was intended to be the third lunar landing, but the mission was aborted after an oxygen tank exploded and crippled the service module. When the threat of being stranded in space became a real one for the astronauts, Mission Control scrambled to devise a rescue plan.

In the movie, as the suspense builds, a frustrated and exhausted Flight Director named Gene Kranz, played by Ed Harris, famously announces to his crew, "Failure is not an option!" It's a powerful line. In fact, the real Gene Kranz went on to use it as the title for his autobiography. Technically, Kranz never uttered those exact words. A crew member had made a similar statement, and it inspired the writers of the screenplay. Either way, it was this sentiment that propelled every man forward at Mission Control. And (SPOILER ALERT) the astronauts never landed on the moon, but they were saved.

Here's the thing: In the end, *Apollo 13* hasn't been remembered as a mission that failed. It was classified as a "successful failure" because the astronauts returned home safely. And I like the sound of that. *Successful failure.*

Life is all about learning how to fail successfully. It's full of risks, and failing can get messy. I'm not sure why some people are able to go with the flow of failure easier than others. Maybe it's their temperament, or they've simply had more experience with losing. But for those of us who invest emotionally (which as far as I'm concerned, if something is worth investing in, why wouldn't you invest emotionally?), failing seems twice as messy. And I like tidy. My brain prefers tidy. It likes things to run smoothly. It likes to run in the comfort zone.

The Whole Ball of Wax

My trouble began on a very frigid January day. I was away at school in my junior year of college when I began to sense that something wasn't right. Looking back, I'd had a few "breakthrough" symptoms. But it wasn't until I felt a lightning bolt of adrenaline shoot through my body that I knew something was seriously wrong. I was terrified. I felt disoriented and remember thinking, *I'm having a heart attack. This is what dying feels like.* But I didn't die, and that's when I began to fear something worse. *Maybe I'm losing my mind.*

The attacks grew worse over time. They were random and relentless and left me waiting for the next ambush. I struggled to complete my studies and lived in self-preservation mode. I hid behind locked doors and withdrew from my friends. My dad picked me up every weekend and brought me home, like a child who couldn't make it through camp.

I remember calling my mom on a particularly bad night and her sharing Paul's words with me and Psalm 34. I found some solace in them but no real answers. I had no peace. And contentment wasn't even on my radar. I made regular trips to the infirmary, but when the doctors and counselors couldn't give me any real answers, they called it stress . . . the great catch-all.

During the next weeks and months, I began scouring articles and medical journals. Ironically, I'd changed from a party girl to a scholar almost overnight. I was desperate to find some disease or disorder I could squeeze myself into. But nothing fit, and I was forced to endure the oppressive silence that comes when the answers won't.

That's when I began to turn things in on myself. I began to think that maybe I was just one of those people who wasn't very strong or didn't have enough faith. I began a series of phobic behaviors, avoiding crowds, loud music, caffeine, and the evening news. It was all too troubling. I wondered if maybe I had offended God. Maybe He wasn't real. Maybe I wasn't real. So I pleaded, "If You're there, please don't let me lose my mind."

It's strange looking back now, because in that moment, there were no voices or flashes of light. But that simple prayer I uttered set things into motion I couldn't have imagined. Somehow I finished school and even married the boy who'd stuck with me through it all. When we relocated to

Milwaukee, I was determined to make a fresh start, even with my odd behaviors. I'd heard about a large metropolitan church in the area and decided I'd force myself to visit the women's group when I could. Even as I continued to struggle physically and mentally, spiritually I knew something was changing.

Scripture from my childhood came flooding back with new texture and form. Maybe God is good, and not because of what He can do for me, but because His nature demands it—even when we hurt, even when things don't fit. One morning, a coordinator

> *Sometimes obeying God is about crashing and burning and then allowing Him to make something beautiful from the ashes.*

approached me and asked if I'd be interested in sharing with the others what I was learning. "Nothing big," she said. "Just ten minutes or so." I stood there for a moment, frozen somewhere between shock and flattery. Then before anyone could stop me, I said, "Yes."

Yes? Are you serious!

As I walked to my car, I wondered if this time I really had lost my mind. How could I have agreed to speak in front of a group of people? I'd been going to great lengths to keep my humiliating affliction private. Standing in front of two hundred women was bound to make things a little trickier.

For a week, I was a woman possessed. I was frightened out of my mind at the prospect of speaking, but I wanted to do it. Somehow, I wanted to share what I was learning about trusting God and what that *really* looks like. It's messy, at times, and even painful. And His timing often leaves something to be desired. I was learning that to live life God's way and embracing His principles didn't always mean I'd look good or feel good in the process. Sometimes obeying God is about crashing and burning and then allowing Him to make something beautiful from the ashes.

We weren't left without a promise. God's hand will pull everything together, right every wrong, and carry us forward.

I prepared for my ten minutes with a vengeance, even while I prayed for flood or pestilence to strike. But Thursday morning dawned sunny and bright, so I gathered up my notes and headed for the door. Just then, the phone rang. It was a woman from church whom I'd never met. She'd seen my name in the bulletin and said she'd been praying for me. She even said she had a Bible verse she wanted to give to me. I was in a hurry, but I thanked her and jotted down the reference. I decided to take a moment and flip through my Bible to the Book of Acts. There I read, "Do not be afraid; keep on speaking, do not be silent. For I am with you" (Acts 18:9-10).

I gave my little talk and heard it went well. All I remember is feeling relieved and being told I was gifted.

I sobbed the whole way home.

When I told my husband what had happened, he tried to convince me to give one more doctor a try. I agreed, but I was reluctant because doctors had done little to help relieve my anxiety in the past.

When I walked into the doctor's office, I knew not to get my hopes up again. I decided I'd try a new approach. I wouldn't tell him why I'd come in. If he was worth the diplomas that hung on his wall, he'd tell me. The doctor listened through his stethoscope, then he paused and asked, "Have you ever been bothered by a racing pulse or anxiety?" *Seriously?* Then he asked if I'd ever had a panic attack.

I was blown away. That's when the floodgates opened, and he handed me tissues while I told him my story. He explained what was happening and put me on heart medication. That very day, my thirteen-year nightmare came to an end.

The Promise

Here's the thing: My lack of peace or contentment wasn't because I was weak or because I had no faith. It wasn't only in my mind or in my spirit. It was organic and involved my body first and foremost, as I'm convinced most "mental illnesses" do. Today, as an author and speaker, I'm often asked where I got my training. And at the risk of sounding uber-spiritual, I tell people it was out in the desert with Moses . . . circling but never quite reaching the Promised Land.

Why did it take the Israelites forty years to do what

should have taken them a month? I had spent thirteen years searching for answers, and the doctor who changed my life was less than two miles from my home. God knew when it was time for the Israelites, and He knew when it was time for me. He was preparing me for something important, and I'm now grateful He didn't cut corners. In fact, my entire perspective on the power of gratitude has changed immensely.

Sure, things get tough, and life can be disappointing. But months after I was diagnosed and treated, I asked my husband how he found the doctor who changed my life. Careful research? good referrals? fasting and praying? Not quite.

As a corporate sales rep for Andersen Windows, he needed to find a physician for his annual checkups. One day, while driving near our new home, he spotted a medical building built with Andersen windows. He went inside, made an appointment, and the rest is history.

Amazing, but this is the stuff contentment is made of. It's not about the bad day, the epic failure, or the utter despair. Trouble will come. We are warned about that. It's evidence of a world that's complex and full of choices we all must make. But we weren't left without a promise. God's hand will pull everything together, right every wrong, and carry us forward.

"'For I know the plans I have for you,' declares the LORD, 'plans to prosper you and not to harm you, plans to give you hope and a future'" (Jeremiah 29:11).

That's contentment.

ACKNOWLEDGMENTS

It's hard to know where to begin or end my thank-yous. So many people have invested in me, and my appreciation is endless.

To my parents, John and Lois, my husband, Sully, my siblings Jay and Lynn, my brother-in-law, Mike, and my kids Matt and Alissa. They've all put up with me, taught me, and encouraged me.

To my daughter-in-law, Kaci, who supplies both friendship and the delight of a growing family. To my nieces and nephews, specifically Kelly and Courtney whose babies filled my empty arms with hours of joy by believing my bedtime songs sounded as good as Mary Poppins.

To my friends George and Kris, John and Susan, and Juan and Becky for extending the helping hand I needed most and for loving me without judgment.

Thank you to my agent, Bob Hostetler, for encouraging and correcting me, and to my new friends at Abingdon Press for believing in me.

Then there are those I've never met but who've impacted

me immensely. Such as the brilliant Oxford Professor John Lennox who embodies the John Hutchinson quote: "An unthinking faith is a curious offering to be made to the creator of the human mind."

To them and to all the others I'd never have enough space to name, thank you.

NOTES

1. The Battle Begins

1. Cal Fussman, "What I've Learned: Woody Allen," *Esquire* (September 2013): 190.

2. Rob Stein, "In Reversal, Death Rates Rise for Middle-Aged Whites," NPR, November 2, 2015, www.npr.org/sections/health-shots/2015/11/02/453192132/in-reversal-death-rates-rise-for-middle-aged-whites.

2. Too Much Drama

1. Chonda Pierce, "I'm a Comedian and I'm Depressed," Anxiety and Depression Association of America, https://adaa.org/living-with-anxiety/personal-stories/im-comedian-and-im-depressed.

2. David Szpilman, MD, et al., " 'Dry Downing' and Other Myths," *Cleveland Clinic Journal of Medicine*, July 1, 2018, www.mdedge.com/ccjm/article/168988/emergency-medicine/dry-drowning-and-other-myths.

3. What Are You Waiting For?

1. Kate Bowler, "Death, the Prosperity Gospel and Me," *New York Times*, February 13, 2016, www.nytimes.com/2016/02/14/opinion/sunday/death-the-prosperity-gospel-and-me.html.

4. Head Games

1. Emma Perez-Trevino, "Remembering Mark J. Kilroy," *The Brownsville* (Texas) *Herald*, March 7, 2009, www.brownsvilleherald.com/news/local/remembering-mark-j-kilroy/article_dfad19e2-ad2b-51a9-8f49-a3a38dd7939f.html.

6. Check Your Judgment at the Door

1. Svend Brinkmann, *Stand Firm: Resisting the Self-Improvement Craze* (Cambridge: Polity, 2014), 86.

2. Jane E. Brody, "A Positive Outlook May Be Good for Your Health," *New York Times*, March 27, 2017, www.nytimes.com/2017 /03/27/well/live/positive-thinking-may-improve-health-and-extend-life .html.

3. Ann C. Sullivan, *Permission to Doubt*, Study Guide (Grand Rapids, MI: Kregel), Lesson 1.

4. Nadine Burke Harris, "How Does Trauma Affect a Child's DNA?" *TED Radio Hour*, part 3 of the episode "Hardwired," August 25, 2017, www.npr.org/2017/08/25/545092982/nadine-burke-harris-how-does -trauma-affect-a-childs-dna.

7. Trendsetters

1. Marguerite Ward, "Tony Robbins Shares a 2-Step Strategy for Feeling More in Control of Your Life," CNBC, July 22, 2017, www .cnbc.com/2017/07/22/tony-robbins-shares-a-2-step-strategy-for-feeling -more-in-control-of-your-life.html.

2. Peter Rowe, "Truly, Madly, Deeply Deepak Chopra," *The San Diego Union-Tribune*, May 3, 2014, www.sandiegouniontribune.com/lifestyle /people/sdut-truly-madly-deepak-chopra-2014may03-htmlstory.html.

3. Ryan Kohls, "Ravi Zacharias," *What I Wanna Know* (blog), March 9, 2012, http://whatiwannaknow.com/2012/03/ravi-zacharias/.

4. Joseph Mazur, "The Myth of Coincidences and Why We Search for Their Meaning," interview by Shankar Vedantam, *Hidden Brain* (podcast), NPR, May 8, 2017, www.npr.org/2016/09/27/495671322/the -myth-of-coincidences-and-why-we-search-for-their-meaning.

8. Making Fear Work

1. Mark A. Smith, "Intolerance, Leadership and Risk-Management," Management Issues website, January 24, 2012, www.management-issues .com/opinion/6390/intolerance-leadership-and-risk-taking/.

2. Ben Casnocha, "Michael Lewis: Do You Know Your Calling?" *Ben

Casnocha (blog), December 10, 2008, http://casnocha.com/2008/12 /michael-lewis-do-you-want-a-job-or-a-calling.html.

3. Alvin Plantinga, "Why Darwinist Materialism Is Wrong," *The New Republic*, November 16, 2012, https://newrepublic.com/article/110189 /why-darwinist-materialism-wrong.

4. John Calvin, *Institutes of the Christian Religion*, vol. 1, trans. Henry Beveridge (Edinburgh: Calvin Translation Society, 1845), 55, 58.

5. Immanuel Kant, *The Critique of Pure Reason*, trans. J. M. D. Meiklejohn (Digireads.com, 2018).

6. John Lennox, "Has Science Buried God?" Copernicus Center for Interdisciplinary Studies, YouTube video, 53:53, July 13, 2015, www .youtube.com/watch?v=PqbZorL-Ysc.

10. Take Back Control

1. Christopher Ryan, "Are We Designed to Be Sexual Omnivores?" TEDx, 13:59, February 2013, www.ted.com/talks/christopher_ryan_are _we_designed_to_be_sexual_omnivores?language=en.

11. Hope Springs Anew

1. Justin Brown, "Harvard Scientist Reveals the Shocking Impact of Watching Porn," Ideapod, April 4, 2014, https://ideapod.com/harvard -scientist-reveals-shocking-impact-watching-porn/.

12. Finding the Purpose

1. Rick Warren, *The Purpose Driven Life* (Grand Rapids: Zondervan, 2002).

13. Toolbox

1. Dr. Seth J. Gillihan, "How Helping Others Can Relieve Anxiety and Depression," *Psychology Today*, October 10, 2017, www .psychologytoday.com/us/blog/think-act-be/201710/how-helping -others-can-relieve-anxiety-and-depression.

ABOUT THE AUTHOR

Ann C. Sullivan has encouraged thousands of people as a celebrated author, international speaker, blogger, and freelance writer. Her articles have been included in *Christianity Today* and *Relevant* magazine. Sullivan's fresh approach and sharp delivery tackle tough topics and find humor in weighty issues.

Sullivan is also an active speaker, empowering men and women in their personal and professional lives. She is a researcher who specializes in anxiety disorders. She graduated from Northern Illinois University where she studied education, history, and philosophy, but it was in the trenches that she gained her most valuable insights.

Sullivan worked for more than ten years coordinating women's studies outside of Milwaukee before expanding her speaking to include the corporate world. She remains passionate about inspiring men and women in all areas of their lives. Read more at anncsullivan.com